The Insider's
Guide to the
Peace Corps

The Insider's Guide to the Peace Corps

What to Know Before You Go

SECOND EDITION

Dillon Banerjee

TEN SPEED PRESS
Berkeley | Toronto

Ten Speed Press
PO Box 7123
Berkeley, California 94707
www.tenspeed.com

Distributed in Australia by Simon and Schuster Australia, in Canada by Ten Speed Press Canada, in New Zealand by Southern Publishers Group, in South Africa by Real Books, and in the United Kingdom and Europe by Publishers Group UK.

Cover and text design by Chloe Rawlins

Previously published as *So, You Want to Join the Peace Corps* (Ten Speed Press, 2000)

Library of Congress Cataloging-in-Publication Data
Banerjee, Dillon.
  The insider's guide to the Peace Corps : what to know before you go /
Dillon Banerjee. — 2nd ed.
      p. cm.
  Rev. ed. of: So, you want to join the Peace Corps. c2000.
  Includes index.
  Summary: "A guide that tells potential Peace Corps volunteers what to expect, through first-hand advice from recent volunteers"—Provided by publisher.
  ISBN 978-1-58008-970-8
  1. Peace Corps (U.S.)—Handbooks, manuals, etc. I. Banerjee, Dillon. So, you want to join the Peace Corps. II. Title.
  HC60.5.B34 2009
  361.6—dc22

                         2008043720

Printed in the United States of America on recycled paper (30% PCW)

First printing this edition, 2009
1 2 3 4 5 6 7 8 9 10 — 13 12 11 10 09

Contents

I. Pre-Application Jitters

II. How to Pack for a Two-Year Trip

III. Peace Corps Training—Learning the Ropes

IV. Managing Your Money

V. Living Like the Locals

VI. Common Medical and Safety Concerns

VII. Staying in Touch with Home

VIII. Peace Corps Gadgets and Technology

IX. The Social Scene

X. The Toughest Job You'll Ever Love?

XI. Rules to Live By—Peace Corps Policy

XII. Traveling Like a Pro

XIII. Post–Peace Corps

Appendices

Acknowledgments

I am grateful to Ten Speed Press for recognizing that the time was right for a second edition, and for convincing me that an update was possible from a continent away. Many thanks and much credit goes to Lindsey McKay, my research assistant, who through her innovative and effective research and analysis techniques helped provide the core data I needed for the rewrite. Thanks as well to my editor at Ten Speed Press, Sara Golski, for her expert guidance. I also want to thank those who provided me with insight into the latest from Peace Corps headquarters (you know who you are!) and the many RPCVs who responded to the surveys and calls for input.

Peace Corps Acronyms

APCD	Associate Peace Corps Director
CED	Community Economic Development
CD	Country Director
COS	Close of Service
EMA	Europe/Mediterranean/Asia Region
ET	Early Termination
HCN	Host Country National
IAP	Inter-America/Pacific Region
IST	In-Service Training
NCE	Noncompetitive Eligibility
NGO	Nongovernmental Organization
PC	Peace Corps
PCMO	Peace Corps Medical Officer
PCT	Peace Corps Trainee
PCV	Peace Corps Volunteer
PCVL	Peace Corps Volunteer Leader
PIP	Performance Improvement Plan
RPCV	Returned Peace Corps Volunteer
TEFL	Teaching English as a Foreign Language
TOT	Training of Trainers

Preface

When Ten Speed Press asked me to update this book for a second edition, I was initially hesitant. I wrote the first book, having just completed my two-year tour as a volunteer in Cameroon, with a wealth of experiential knowledge that was fresh, pertinent, and ripe for sharing. Detailing the "Peace Corps experience" was a reliance more on memory than research, and there was little about the Peace Corps world that I felt was unknown to me—from the application process right through to job searching post–Peace Corps.

Nine years later, however, I felt sure that the Peace Corps had evolved to a point where it would be far less familiar to me. I knew, for example, that the application process had migrated online, that volunteers the world over had cell phones, that Peace Corps–issued motorcycles were a thing of the past, and that PCVs were as likely to be teaching GIS mapping and website development as digging fishponds or planting trees. To make the proposition of an update even more daunting, I was living thirty-five hundred miles away from the United States, not scheduled to return until 2011 when my assignment to the U.S. Embassy in Portugal was complete.

All the same, the publisher insisted that a second edition would serve as an important resource for new and prospective Peace Corps applicants and that much of the core research could be done remotely. With invaluable input from my research assistant, Lindsey McKay, an RPCV who served in the Dominican Republic from 2004 to 2006, I started collecting information on today's Peace Corps. As I analyzed feedback from RPCV discussion groups and interviews, and combed through the latest statistics, policy manuals, volunteer handbooks, surveys, and websites, I began to realize that, in actuality, very little of the Peace Corps volunteer experience had changed over the past decade. There may be new ways to apply, new gadgets to pack, and new rules to follow, but PCVs the world over go through the same basic stages of orientation, adjustment, and integration that has defined the experience since the inception of the organization over forty years ago.

So—why should you read this book? As with the first edition, my core motivation was to furnish prospective Peace Corps volunteers with a comprehensive resource that will help unravel what is still a largely mysterious and daunting work and life commitment. Despite a plethora of new websites, blogs, and multimedia snippets where individual volunteers share their thoughts, fears, or daily lives in country X or program Y, there is still a surprising lack of information tailored to someone who just wants to know what it's like to be a Peace Corps volunteer—period. Life throughout the developing world shares a surprising number of commonalities when it comes to basics like health, safety, infrastructure, and transportation. And life overseas as an expatriate entails basic adjustments to culture, society, and environment that cannot be avoided. All of these areas and related experiences are detailed in this book, along with many more. You should find the information provided in the following pages helpful regardless of whether you end up teaching English in Mali or training entrepreneurs in Bulgaria. As with the first edition, the information is provided in a straightforward, question-and-answer format, but now includes the latest on everything from the online application process and what to pack to safety considerations and staying in touch with home.

Deciding to join the Peace Corps and live overseas for two years is not easy. The greatest hurdle is often a mental one: stepping into the unknown and hoping to find the strength, commitment, and flexibility to see it though. I hope the information here will put things into perspective and allow you to consider the Peace Corps in a less intimidating light. Regardless of what you decide, I hope you continue to pursue ways to help make this world a better one, all the while seeking adventure and fun in your life.

Happy trails,
Dillon

Part I

Pre-Application Jitters

1

What is the application process like? How long does it take?

The application process can be arduous and seemingly endless. The Peace Corps receives over two hundred thousand inquiries each year from people interested in applying. Tens of thousands of those people submit applications, and only a fraction is eventually accepted. Besides the fact that the Peace Corps is a government agency—which, by definition, means it can be slow and bureaucratic—the sheer number of applicants combined with the excruciating detail each must provide on the application forms make it easy to understand why the review process can last up to a year.

The Peace Corps tells potential recruits that three personality traits are invaluable during the application process: persistence, patience, and a sense of humor. Persistence is required because, try as they may, the Peace Corps does not always review every application and forward every file in a timely manner. Every so often you'll need to prod and encourage them to keep the process moving. I knew an applicant who, after submitting his completed application, sat back and waited to hear from the Peace Corps. He never followed up with calls; he never thought to check on the status of his application. After almost six months of waiting, he received a letter notifying him that his application had been deemed "inactive." Apparently, having never heard from him, his recruiter assumed he had lost interest in joining.

Patience is a virtue for Peace Corps applicants simply because, even if you are persistent and hound the office with weekly calls, the entire process may take anywhere from four to twelve months. Why does it take so long? Because there are several steps one must take to navigate successfully through the system. In a nutshell, they are:

1. Filling out the application. This is no easy feat, though it has been made a bit less cumbersome now that the entire process can be completed online. From Peace Corps' official website (www.peacecorps.gov), you can create an account that allows you to access the application and complete it in stages at your convenience. You can also track your progress so you know where you are in the process at any given time. That said, the application still consists of seventeen distinct sections ranging from queries on personal and legal information to military status, language skills, and employment history. The Peace Corps demands an account of every relevant course, internship, summer job, and hobby that may qualify you for one of their programs. You must provide three references (one professional, one personal, and one from a volunteer work supervisor) and write two five hundred-word essays (detailing your motivation to apply, and any past cross-cultural experiences). The Office of Personnel Management (OPM) estimates that the Peace Corps application should take approximately eight hours to complete. In reality, expect to be filling in the blanks for days, if not weeks, due to the amount and depth of information requested. If you are unable to access or complete the forms online, you can request that Peace Corps send you hard copies so you can put pen to paper.

2. Passing an interview. Once your application has been reviewed, the Peace Corps determines whether or not you "fit" into any of their program areas. If you do, you will be called into the nearest Peace Corps office for an interview with a recruiter. If you are unable to attend in person, the interview may be conducted over the phone. This step of the process is a major screening tool for the Peace Corps. It is their forum for evaluating your level of commitment, maturity, and experience, and it is your golden opportunity to sell yourself, your skills, and your ambition. During the interview, expect to be grilled on your reasons

for wanting to join, your expectations, your hopes and fears, your strengths and weaknesses, and your preferences with regard to the Peace Corps' geographic and program areas. They may also ask you whether or not you are dating anyone seriously—a red flag to help them identify volunteers who may quit before their two-year commitments are fulfilled (see questions 59 and 60 for more on early termination [ET]).

You should treat the interview as you would any other job interview. Be professional, confident, assertive, and prepared. Many applicants assume they can wear shorts and a T-shirt, or show up without preparation since it's an interview for the Peace Corps. Recruiters will be turned off by that. They are not looking for applicants who come across as extremely liberal or laid-back; they're looking for the best-qualified applicants among thousands of competitors.

3. Securing a nomination. Assuming the interview goes well, your recruiter will "nominate" you for one of the Peace Corps' programs. Possibilities include education, youth outreach, community development, business development, environment, agriculture, health, HIV/AIDS, and information technology. For a complete description of Peace Corps programs, refer to appendix C. If you aren't slotted for a program that interests you, this would be the time to speak with your recruiter about revisiting your qualifications as they may relate to other programs.

You'll also be told the region of the world in which you will most likely serve, the language requirements for that region, and your approximate date of departure. On the one hand, receiving such information boosts your morale and provides exciting news for friends and family. On the other hand, once the initial impact wears off, impatience and frustration tend to grow. You'll quickly realize how much of the picture is still missing. You won't know the exact country assignment, the actual date of departure, the specific language(s) you'll be learning, or the details of the projects you will be working on. This is usually the stage that applicants find the most trying.

4. Physical and legal screening. Step 4 is when you undergo a thorough medical, dental, and legal review, while the Peace Corps checks on all of your references and validates the information provided on your application. The physical, dental, and eye exams can all be conducted by your regular doctors; costs are reimbursed by the Peace Corps. Legal clearances include an FBI background check and a closer look at issues related to financial obligations or debts, dependents, and marital status.

During this stage, your recruiter will also keep his or her eyes peeled for specific openings that suit your qualifications. Timing is everything at this point. If your medical exams go off without a hitch, hound the office to ensure that Peace Corps nurses review your file in a timely manner. Call your recruiter frequently to follow the progress of your background and reference check, and inquire about his or her efforts to place your name in an available and appropriate volunteer slot.

5. Receiving an invitation. The last stage of the application process is receiving the coveted "invitation" for a specific program, in a specific country, leaving on a specific day. You will be invited, for example, to teach English as a second language in Niger, leaving August 3. You'll have only ten days to accept the invitation, so do some quick research and some serious soul-searching to be sure that you are committed and willing to go.

If you have doubts about the country to which you've been assigned—perhaps it's predominantly French-speaking, Muslim, and urban, whereas you had your hopes set on Spanish-speaking, animist, and rural—you may want to inquire about other possibilities. Be sure, though, that your doubts are substantial and reasonable, not impulsive or superficial, and communicate them clearly to your recruiter. If you bow out of your initial invitation because you've heard the food stinks and the beaches are dirty, you're likely not to receive another invitation down the line. If you feel your reasons are solid, however, consult your recruiter and ask about other possibilities opening in the near future that may be more in line with your desires and expectations. Stay flexible, and don't come across as demanding.

Throughout the application process, remember to maintain a sense of humor. As I mentioned earlier, you're battling a bureaucracy that is deluged annually with paperwork. They deserve kudos for managing to process as much as they do, but to an eager applicant whose life hinges on their decisions, each snag along the way can lead to a nervous breakdown. If you learn to laugh when you'd rather scream, you'll be more likely to emerge from the application process unscathed.

When you finally accept an invitation, you can breathe a huge sigh of relief and start spreading the word that you're going overseas to be a Peace Corps volunteer! You can begin reading up on your new country, contacting RPCVs who served there to ask them questions about their experiences and preparing your belongings for a unique packing effort (see question 11). You will have reached the end of a long and winding road, and should enjoy it before the beginning of a much longer and more winding road begins—the actual Peace Corps experience itself! Spend the intervening months between the invitation and departure doing all the things you need and want to do, knowing that it may be two years before you get the chance to do those things again. Say your good-byes, see your favorite band, go to the latest movie, eat your favorite foods, visit good friends, and spend quality time with family. All the while, cherish the fact that you have been selected to embark on an adventure that few others have the privilege of experiencing in their lifetimes, and know that you are about to discover new things about the world, about others, and about yourself.

2
Am I qualified to join the Peace Corps?

The Peace Corps is asked this question frequently, and as a result has published a pamphlet entitled "Life is calling. How far will you go?" This resource provides an overview of Peace Corps' various program areas, along with the educational and experiential requirements applicants should meet to be considered for each one. I have included the overview as appendix C in this book to give you an idea of the skills needed for accomplishing projects within each program. I also, however, highly recommend that you request the full pamphlet from your local recruiting office, as it goes into greater detail on program prerequisites and desired qualifications.

In addition to specific program requirements, be aware of a few core requirements all applicants must meet before joining the Peace Corps. Volunteers must, for example, be U.S. citizens at least eighteen years old and in good health (there is no upper age limit). Most PCVs (95 percent) have bachelor's degrees, and several have advanced degrees and/or related prior work experience. Married couples with dependent children are generally not accepted into the Peace Corps unless there is a compelling need for their specific skills; those without dependents may be accepted if both qualify for volunteer assignments (see question 3). All applicants must undergo a comprehensive medical and dental evaluation certifying that they are capable of handling the physical and emotional rigors of Peace Corps service.

When completing the application forms, be sure to include every bit of related experience that comes to mind. Oftentimes applicants don't realize how important it is to be absolutely and completely thorough. If you spent a summer helping your mom with gardening in the backyard, you may qualify for the Peace Corps' agriculture or forestry program. If you took a CPR course as part of your Boy Scout merit badge, you may be selected for the health education program. If you took two years of high school Spanish, volunteered for a few days at a food shelter, or organized a backcountry camping expedition with your friends, include it on your application. Roughly 50 percent of PCVs hold liberal arts degrees, which means their technical experience often comes from extracurricular activities, summer jobs, or personal hobbies. No matter how trivial or inane some of your previous experiences may seem to you, if it sounds even remotely related to a Peace Corps program, jot it down.

3

What if I'm married and we both want to join?

Go for it! Peace Corps statistics show that 7 percent of all volunteers are married. There is even an official one-pager entitled "Joining Peace Corps as a Couple," which addresses the application process, eligibility, and preparation for service (see appendix J). There were a few married Peace Corps volunteers in Cameroon during my time there. One couple had recently retired and were serving as teachers in a vocational school; another were newlyweds who had decided to join the Peace Corps before having kids, mortgages, and all that good stuff. From my observations, both had good experiences and were glad they joined. If you are married and are considering the Peace Corps, though, you should be aware of a few things.

First, the application process can be much longer for married couples. The Peace Corps places volunteers by matching program needs, as determined by requests from host country governments, with the skills of its applicants. Placing two people in the same country simultaneously requires requests from a country for volunteers under both programs for which the two qualify. In other words, if you are nominated to be an agroforestry volunteer and your spouse is slated for the health program, you must wait until a country has openings for both and hope that you can fill those spots simultaneously. There may also be complications if the training schedules for your programs are not synchronized. It may be that agroforestry in-country training starts in June, while health training doesn't start until September. These are just some of the kinks married couples face that may take the Peace Corps some time to iron out.

The Peace Corps will also want you to be aware that, if you are married, you may be tempted to lean more on your spouse than on other volunteers or villagers for support, guidance, and companionship. Although, to a degree, this is natural and expected, if taken to an extreme it can result in couples feeling isolated from peers, counterparts, neighbors, and friends. Tensions can also arise if one spouse acculturates more easily, proves more adept at learning languages, or is more technically proficient than the other. These tensions may be exacerbated in newlyweds who haven't yet had the chance to mature in their marriages. Perhaps for this reason, married couples have a slightly higher ET rate than single volunteers, which is something to bear in mind. Don't be discouraged, however, as the majority of married couples in the Peace Corps have served successfully and rewardingly. My advice is to contact the Peace Corps or send out inquiries on the Internet to communicate with returned volunteers who served with their spouses, and ask them about their experiences and for their counsel.

4

Can I serve in the Peace Corps with my boyfriend or girlfriend?

No. The only way to enter the Peace Corps with a partner and be posted in the same village is to be married. Otherwise there are no guarantees that the two of you will even end up on the same continent. In fact, if you are involved in a serious relationship, be aware that the Peace Corps will inquire about the nature of that relationship during the application process. If they perceive it to be potentially problematic, they may have you complete a Romantic Involvement Worksheet used to "educate" applicants on the ways in which a Peace Corps commitment can strain personal relationships (see appendix I). If they conclude that your emotional attachment is substantial, it will count as a strike against you. This is because a significant number of people who early terminate do so as a direct result of feeling homesick for their boyfriends or girlfriends. Many people get so wrapped up in the adventurous and romantic notion of becoming a Peace Corps volunteer in a foreign country, that they underestimate the feelings of isolation, loneliness, and insecurity that arise from time to time during the experience—feelings that may be compounded if the volunteer has left someone special back home. Most volunteers I know who left a boyfriend or girlfriend behind to join the Peace Corps were not in those relationships two years down the road. Distance and time are two skilled assassins of even the strongest bonds, and in the Peace Corps, they tend to be armed and dangerous.

5

What will my Peace Corps experience be like if I'm an "older" volunteer?

Approximately 5 percent of Peace Corps volunteers are over the age of fifty (see appendix A). I served with several older volunteers in Cameroon, and they absolutely loved it. In fact, in many ways they seemed to have an easier time with the adjustments and hurdles that their younger colleagues often stumbled through. They were more directed, more assured of their reasons for being overseas, more open to meeting new people and experiencing new hardships, and more comfortable with relinquishing the luxuries of life in the States. Often they had thought about joining the Peace Corps for years beforehand and came with professional skills that could be readily and effectively applied to their program areas. In addition, older PCVs in many countries, simply because of their age, enjoy an inherent level of respect and authority from colleagues, program administrators, and host country nationals (HCNs) in general. This "automatic" respect, which younger volunteers spend months (if not years) earning, greatly facilitates their adjustment to life and work overseas.

If you are an older applicant and have concerns about joining, the best thing to do is call the Peace Corps and speak with a recruiter. He or she can tell you the most common age-related issues regarding Peace Corps service and put you in touch with other RPCVs who are happy to discuss their experiences with you. Peace Corps has also dedicated a section of their website to "50+" volunteers, which includes vignettes from PCVs who have served in various parts of the world and lists frequently asked questions—some of which I have included in appendix K. You will have to undergo a more thorough (or at least time-consuming) medical examination, and tying up loose ends stateside before leaving may be more involved, but aside from that, the application process will be no different.

One issue older volunteers are often forewarned about is the "surrogate parent" syndrome they may face during training and, to a limited extent, during their entire two years. Moving overseas can be an unnerving ordeal, often transforming brazen college graduates into callow youths. When this happens, to whom do the youths reflexively turn for solace and comfort? The person who most reminds them of Mom or Dad. If the older volunteer isn't careful, he or she may end up playing parent for thirty angst-ridden college grads, depriving him– or herself of an otherwise culturally enriching and personally rewarding transition into life in the developing world.

Older volunteers may also initially feel uncomfortable with the fact that the bulk of their support group is much younger than they are. They may feel out of place during Peace Corps parties, which are typically hosted by younger volunteers and more closely resemble college bashes than placid social gatherings. During training, they may find themselves distanced from younger volunteers who are able to pick up languages more easily. Over time, however, everyone (young and old) finds their niche and settles into a pace of life and social interaction that they feel comfortable with. The older PCVs in my program ended up forging close and lasting friendships with people half their age, finding common ground in shared experiences and mutual support.

6

What will my Peace Corps experience be like if I'm gay?

Gay volunteers can generally expect to find support from Peace Corps administration and fellow PCVs. In many countries, organized support networks exist for gay and lesbian volunteers; in others it's less formal, but you can usually find support if you need or want it. The topic is covered in diversity sessions during training, and the environment within the Peace Corps community is often open and accepting. That isn't to say that every volunteer in the Peace Corps is open-minded about homosexuality. The volunteer community is, in some ways, a microcosm of society in the States and therefore includes its share of homophobic and intolerant people. For the most part, though, expect an understanding and judgment-free environment.

The same cannot be said, however, for life in the village. In many parts of the developing world, homosexuality is either unrecognized (considered not to exist) or is thought of as abnormal and even insane behavior. Gay volunteers often have to gauge the social climate of their posts and decide on an individual basis whether they feel comfortable telling local friends and neighbors about themselves. Many gay volunteers feel pressure at their posts to act heterosexual in social situations, knowing that to do otherwise could have serious repercussions on their work and social lives. There are instances where volunteers meet gay members of the local community and date them, but rarely are those relationships made public. So be forewarned: as intolerant as society may sometimes seem in the States, it's even worse in most other parts of the world. There will, however, be support available to you from the Peace Corps administration, friends, and other volunteers, and it needn't prevent you from having a successful and fulfilling two years overseas.

For perspectives and anecdotes from lesbian and gay PCVs around the world, as well as from applicants and even a former Peace Corps recruiter, check out the LGBT Peace Corps Alumni website at www.lgbrpcv.org/articles.htm.

7

What will my Peace Corps experience be like if I'm a minority?

The most trying aspect of the Peace Corps experience for minority volunteers may be dealing with international stereotypes. Oftentimes people's perceptions of the United States are a direct product of imported videos, movies, slogans, and consumer goods. Americans, for example, must be tall, fair-skinned, blond, and blue-eyed. If you don't match that description (at least vaguely), you must not be a "real" American. And even if you surmount the most outlandish stereotypes, you are undoubtedly rich with very important connections in Washington and Hollywood.

To a degree, dispelling these myths is part of your job whether you are a minority volunteer or not. The second goal of the Peace Corps mission statement is, after all, "helping to promote a better understanding of Americans on the part of the peoples served." This includes inculcating the melting pot reality of America into the psyche of your host community. With time, many minority PCVs form deep bonds with their neighbors and counterparts; some even more so than their nonminority Peace Corps peers. Just be aware that the initial reception you receive when you move into your work site may not be the one you had anticipated or envisioned.

You should also be aware that, depending on where you serve, you may actually be the first minority American to interact closely with the local community. In this case, you may be treated as a novelty or even a local star. Conversely some African-American volunteers serving in Africa are surprised to find villagers calling them "white man" and treating them with the aloofness or formality often afforded to white expatriates. Again, approaching the experience with an open and patient mind will generally bear fruit over the long term, regardless of initial reactions.

Incredible as it may seem, another source of frustration for minority volunteers may come from the Peace Corps volunteer community itself. Sadly the Peace Corps microcosm may initially polarize, with non-minority PCVs gravitating toward a social and support network separate from that of minority PCVs. Although such lines inevitably blur, those early instances in which minority volunteers may feel alienated from both the HCN and general PCV community can be overwhelming.

The Peace Corps addresses minority volunteer issues during in-country training diversity sessions. Second-year volunteers visit the training site and give talks, put on skits, and hold discussion groups about life in the Peace Corps as it pertains to minority and racial issues. You will also be able to talk to your program director and Peace Corps volunteer leader (PCVL) if you are encountering any unpleasant situations at post. Your fellow volunteers will be great sounding boards for venting frustrations too. There are some good websites you may wish to peruse prior to joining, such as the Minority Peace Corps Association (www.minoritypca.org/PCStories.html). In all, minority issues are valid and important, but not ones which should prevent you from becoming a Peace Corps Volunteer or having a rewarding experience.

8

Will the two years go by quickly or slowly?

Time is a roller coaster in the Peace Corps. You'll lose track of hours, days, even weeks at some points. Other times will go so slowly you'll think you're in the twilight zone. When work is plentiful and you feel adjusted to village life, days will pass in the blink of an eye. When you hit a lull or endure those inevitable periods of acute homesickness, the spaces between seconds will seem miles wide. On the whole, however, most returned volunteers will tell you that their time spent in the Peace Corps was the fastest two years of their lives.

You'll hear a common theory that your second year goes by much more quickly than your first. Although it's a sweeping generalization, to a degree I think it holds true. Your first year typically starts off with a bang, deceiving you into thinking that the entire two years will fly by regardless of what older, more experienced volunteers say. Everything feels new and exciting, adventurous and challenging. A few months into it, however, as the novelty begins to wear off and the reality of your commitment begins to set in, you realize just how much time you have ahead of you. You may peer into the tunnel convinced that there is no light at the end. The months from the middle to the end of your first year can be painfully slow.

As you commence your second year, however, you'll most likely feel a growing sense of accomplishment and begin to realize how far you've come since swearing in. As you take in the breadth of your successes—with regard to work, life, language, friendships, health, and so on—you'll also gain new perspective, placing greater value on the remaining (and quickly diminishing) time you have left in-country. You will have passed the "hump" (the halfway mark), making your remaining time in the Peace Corps seem to glide by much more smoothly.

To a large extent, the pace of your overseas experience will also depend on your attitude, outlook, and approach. Regardless of where on the curve you stand, the more aware of time you are, the slower it will pass. The more idle and bored you are, the slower it will pass. The more isolated, lonely, and anxious you feel, the slower it will pass. So have fun, realize you're doing something great and finite, be creative with your free time, and strive to get the most out of each passing moment.

9
Will I be lonely?

Yes. At certain points during your service, as you would during any other two-year period of your life regardless of where you were or what you were doing, you will feel lonely. Perhaps the greater question is, "Will I be lonely a lot?" or "Will I get so lonely that it will be unbearable?" Admittedly it really depends on you, your outlook, your personality, and your circumstances. But in most cases, the answer is no.

As a Peace Corps volunteer, certain experiences and concurrent emotions are amplified; the highs are really high, and the lows can be really low. When it's all said and done, however, you'll realize a nice balance was struck during your two years abroad, incorporating some of the most memorable moments of your life—good and bad.

For example, when you find yourself alone at post and you receive a letter from a friend that describes all the fun you are missing back home, the ensuing depression may, at times, seem extreme. Amid all the other hardships you'll face daily, even a pebble of loneliness can sometimes cause an avalanche of anxiety. On the other hand, an occasional wallow in the "lows" affords you the perspective of rejoicing in the "highs." Ironically it's those acute moments of loneliness or feelings of isolation that make the "Peace Corps moments"—those times when you realize you'd rather be nowhere else on earth—so great.

Loneliness is part of the Peace Corps package—part of what makes the experience both meaningful and rewarding when you come out the other end after two years. If you stick through the lonely points, you will experience life in a completely unique and meaningful way. Even if you don't learn much about the things the Peace Corps intends for you to learn, you'll learn a lot about yourself.

As clichéd as this may sound, there is something else that warrants mentioning here: there is a very real difference between feeling lonely and being alone. The longer you serve in the Peace Corps, the more you come to appreciate that difference. Initially you'll link the two together, feeling lonely most intensely when you are alone. But soon you will begin to value your independence and understand that it provides you the opportunity and freedom to enjoy moments that the hectic pace of life in the States denies you. As you become integrated into your village or town, as you make friends with volunteers and host country nationals, as you get comfortable with your work and your new environment, you begin to covet those quiet, deeply personal times alone—times to reflect, to think, to relax, to read, to listen to music, to cook, to write, to sleep. When you get back to the States after it's all over, you'll realize the calming effect that time alone had on your spirit, and it will feel good.

10

What will I miss the most?

You'll get some interesting answers to this question depending on whom you ask. Rather than try to tell you what I think you'll miss the most based on my experiences, I polled recently returned PCVs who served all over the world and lumped their responses together in the paragraph below. I figure this way you'll have a more comprehensive and entertaining picture of the possibilities. Here's what the group came up with, in no particular order:

Pizza, movies, live music, good beer, snow, donuts, driving, happy hour, chips and salsa, hot showers, sofas, friends and family, flush toilets, roomy cars, Twizzlers, Sunday papers, jogging, orange juice, thick mattresses, margaritas, libraries, climate control, milk, cigars, mosquito-free evenings, good water pressure, potable tap water, Hershey's chocolate, real ketchup, privacy, washing machines, shopping malls, Diet Coke, high-speed Internet access, magazine subscriptions, TV, bagels, paved roads, Frosted Flakes, pool tables, ice cream, anonymity, carpeting, egg rolls, coffee shops, bookstores, customer service, deli sandwiches, good batteries, the U.S. Postal Service, down pillows, fine wines.

The list goes on, but I think you get the idea. As several RPCVs pointed out, however, it is truly amazing how creative volunteers get when it comes to improvising or making what they miss or need.

Part II

How to Pack for a Two-Year Trip

11
What should I bring?

I could probably write a whole book on this question alone. The thought of packing only eighty pounds worth of stuff to last you for two years is almost incomprehensible. How is anyone supposed to fit clothing, toiletries, cameras, music, books, toys, pictures, mementos, camping gear, shoes, journals, and so on into two bags and a day pack? And how does one even begin to calculate which items are necessities and which can be left behind?

Packing for the Peace Corps is not as difficult as it seems, but it can be if you're unprepared. Once you find out which country you are going to, you can start researching and making comprehensive lists. You can send out requests for packing suggestions on Peace Corps websites and blogs. You can scan the Peace Corps' recommended packing list included in the Country Profile packet mailed to you (though take it with a grain of salt, as the lists are often outdated). You can call RPCVs who served in the country you'll be in, and pick their brains for hints on what to pack. You'll find that if you use common sense and gather as much information as you can, you'll be packed up and ready quicker than you'd think.

Without going into great detail about specific items to bring, I can provide some general guidelines that I think will prove useful for anyone anxious about packing for the Peace Corps. First, pack light. You will be moving to a different country, culture, and environment—not a different planet. There will be plenty of basic supplies available at local markets, stalls, and shops no matter where you are. Count on finding towels, soap, combs, toilet paper, disposable razors, feminine hygiene products, sheets, pillows, blankets, pots, pans, silverware, various spices, film, batteries, pencils, envelopes, and other staple products locally. In other words, don't stock up on those items—you'll be wasting valuable packing space.

Also, people all over the world wear clothes. There are no Peace Corps villages I know of where the inhabitants literally run around naked all day. This means clothes are available locally—some prêt-à-porter, others made to order. In most developing countries, beautifully patterned cloth and basic textiles of all kinds are available in the markets, and the skills of local tailors often surpass their higher-paid counterparts in the States.

What you may want to bring in the way of clothing are articles that can't be made or purchased easily overseas—items such as GORE-TEX rain gear; strong, durable hiking boots, shoes, and sandals; durable jeans; Thorlo-type socks; a warm wool or fleece sweater; good cotton bras and underwear; quality T-shirts, and so on. You'll also want to pack a set or two of nice clothes (especially true for education, business development, IT, and health volunteers). Many people in developing countries place a high value on appearance and will appreciate it if you dress well. What you bring should also reflect the variations of climate within your country, both seasonally and geographically. In Cameroon, for instance, dry season nights were much cooler and crisper than rainy season nights. Rainy season days were much more moderate than dry season days. And the Northwest and Adamoua provinces were much more mountainous and temperate than the rest of the country. Knowing this before I left the States helped me decide to pack a few warm clothes. Also, I discovered that the summit of Mount Cameroon, at around thirteen thousand feet, frequently dips below freezing. Since I planned on trekking up at some point during my two years, I packed gear that I knew would keep me cozy on that trip.

Aside from clothing, what else should you pack? Most basic toiletries, like I said earlier, will be available locally. You may, however, want to bring a favorite brand of shampoo, conditioner, soap, shaving cream, hair spray, deodorant, or other products that aren't always available overseas. It's best to consult an RPCV from the area to find out exactly which toiletries should make it into your bags.

Many people nowadays wonder about bringing laptops, MP3 players, GPS units, digital cameras, cell phones, and so on. For detailed information on electronics and gadgets in the Peace Corps, skip ahead to part VIII. Speaking generically for packing purposes, however, you will want some kind of portable music player with speakers (not just headphones), adapters for anything you'll need to charge, and a travel-sized transformer for plug-in electronics that are only rated for U.S. current (110–120V). Batteries are available everywhere but may be pricey, so tossing in a few AAs to last you through training is a good idea. Also, make sure your gadgets are well-protected in cushioned and, if possible, watertight cases.

Regardless of whether you like to camp or not, I highly recommend packing a sleeping bag and sleeping pad. You'll find they come in handy when you're visiting other volunteers, when you're traveling to faraway places, and when you have guests come to visit. If you are an avid camper and you plan on taking serious expeditions, bring a camping stove (an "international" model that can run off of multiple fuel sources), a water purifier, and anything else you'd pack for a back-country trip in the States. Normally camping equipment is made to be light and portable, so you'll be able to fit all your camping toys into your bags without sacrificing too much space or weight.

You should definitely bring a book or two of U.S. stamps. As I mention in question 39, you will have plenty of opportunities to hand off letters and small packages to people who are returning to the States. Doing this not only significantly reduces delivery time, but also virtually guarantees that your mail will reach its destination. If, however, your mail is not stamped, you end up inconveniencing the deliverer and risking delay. Stamps weigh virtually nothing and take up practically no space. Just make sure they are the self-adhesive kind, not the ones you have to lick, which gum up in humid climates and end up sticking to each other long before you need them. Stamps are also easily mailed to you in a care package once you run out.

Spices are often cited by volunteers as something they wish they'd brought more of. There are lots of basic spices available everywhere (salt, pepper, garlic, ginger, hot peppers, and so on), but if you have some favorites and aren't sure if they are sold overseas, bring your own supply. Better yet, bring the seeds—you'll have the time and means once you are set up in your village to start a garden or spice patch. After all, the only thing better than good spices are fresh, organically grown, handpicked good spices.

Finally, keep in mind that your country of service will be your home for two years, so save room for items that may not be "necessities" in the traditional sense of the word, but that you wouldn't want to go two years without. This includes pictures, favorite posters, objects of sentimental value, your favorite stuffed animal, and whatever else reminds you of home or makes you feel secure. I also recommend packing a few gifts or souvenirs for host families you may live with during training or when first arriving at your work site—they will be an appreciated gesture and serve as effective icebreakers. If some of these items won't fit in your baggage, don't fret. Remember that you can have items sent to you (especially smaller, less critical ones), and pack accordingly.

12

Can I really pack only eighty pounds to take with me?

Yes and no. The Peace Corps uses something called a Government Excess Baggage Allowance Ticket (GEBAT—since everything out of Washington has to have an acronym). GEBATs authorize Peace Corps trainees to pack two bags of checked luggage with a combined weight of eighty pounds, regardless of normal airline limitations or restrictions. In addition to that, some airlines will also allow a carry-on bag (though others will weigh the carry-ons against the eighty-pound limit, so check in advance). If the Peace Corps has officially designated your post as a "cold climate" assignment, the limit goes up to 102 pounds to accommodate bulkier wardrobes and heavier gear.

Generally speaking, it's a good idea to stay around the eighty-pound mark, but I've found (especially in talking with other PCVs) that it's not exactly a "hard" target. The Peace Corps wants to prevent you from packing everything you own in a panicked effort not to forget anything. If that limit didn't exist, people would walk into the airport with suitcases stuffed with everything from kitchen appliances to gym equipment. Although the weight limit may seem a bit low for a two-year life experience, it keeps you from overdoing it and forces you to prioritize.

That said, many trainees are shocked to see others in their group lugging piles of baggage that clearly surpass the allotted limit by a good ten or twenty pounds. They are even more surprised to see those bags tagged and loaded onto the plane right alongside their sparse and trim lot, with no penalty or consequence. This is because the Peace Corps is often granted a predetermined "group weight limit" for their flights, which must not be surpassed. In other words, as long as some volunteers come in underweight, others can pack overweight loads.

Keeping this in mind, don't fret if you weigh your bags and discover that, with all the paring and trimming, you still come out a little heavy—especially if you've determined that there are no more items you may be able to do without. Odds are no one will notice and a few of your fellow trainees will make up the difference by packing light and, by default, tossing a few extra pounds of allotment your way. In the event that you are strictly held to the eighty-pound limit but you have packed more, you will also have the option of paying for that excess baggage at the airport—but we all know how quickly that can add up.

13

What kinds of games and toys should I bring?

You should bring games you can play by yourself, games that you can easily teach others to play, and small, challenging games that won't bore you easily—for example: cards, Scrabble, Yahtzee, cribbage, a hacky sack, handheld computer games, backgammon, dominoes, and so on. Games are treasured in the Peace Corps, especially in countries where volunteers don't have televisions or movie theaters to rely on for entertainment. Reading can get old and doesn't quite cut it as a social event when you have friends over. Eating, drinking, and conversing are always fun, but when you hit the inevitable lull, games can spice things up.

Besides bringing games for your own entertainment, they serve as excellent icebreakers and kid-pleasers at post. I had some of my greatest laughs in the village teaching Cameroonians how to play American card games and hacky sacking with my neighbors. And when you leave the Peace Corps, all those trinkets and board games make perfect gifts.

14

How many books should I bring?

Books are like movies in the Peace Corps. They are the primary form of escape, entertainment, diversion, distraction, relaxation, and therapy for volunteers worldwide. Never in your life will you have such a devoted opportunity to read as many books as you can and want, to enrich your mind and broaden your thoughts. You will come to view your books as doors to other places, people, and times. And the beauty of it all is that everything is already over there, for the most part.

Volunteers come and go like the wind, and most of them like to pack light. This means that entire libraries collect in Peace Corps offices, rest houses, on volunteers' shelves, and in training centers. And the supply is continuously refreshed by new volunteers, care packages, tourists, and visiting family and friends. So don't worry too much about hauling a mini-library to post with you when you leave the States. You should, however, carefully select a handful of books that you've been dying to read or can't live without, especially newer ones that may not yet be circulating in the volunteer network.

To this day, I remain grateful for the time that I had overseas to fully immerse myself in good literature. Hunting for new books and authors among the dusty shelves of Peace Corps houses around the country was a favorite pastime, and I was happy to leave my personal collection for future volunteers when I COS'd, in order to keep the tradition going.

15

What about the water?
Will I need a purifier?

Do not worry about water. The Peace Corps will teach you all you need to know to prepare water for drinking. They will go over various methods of filtering, boiling, and purifying. You'll learn to disinfect water with chlorine bleach and other solutions. If necessary, you'll also be given a ceramic candle water filter for your house, or money to buy one locally as part of your settling-in allowance.

In addition, as those of you who have traveled extensively already know, bottled water is available in almost every country in the world. Though Peace Corps volunteers usually can't afford bottled water as their primary drinking source, it suffices when they're away from post and unable to treat local water. If you have a portable (camping) water purifier, you may wish to bring it if space allows, but few volunteers use them as alternatives abound.

My strongest recommendation is to maintain vigilant in treating your drinking water throughout your service. I can't count the number of volunteers I knew who, after several months at post, abandoned their water treatment routines. Some wanted to acclimate their systems to local water as a kind of Peace Corps rite of passage. Others were too lazy to boil and filter consistently. Still others falsely assumed their water source was clean due to the location of their posts. Not surprisingly, these were the same volunteers who battled strange stomach disorders and made repeated trips to the medical office for the duration of their service. Though giardia (waterborne amoebas) can usually be treated with a few pills, why expose yourself to the discomfort and health risk in the first place? The Peace Corps' methods for treating water are simple and effective.

As for bathing, many PCVs rely on tubs of water and a cup for dumping the water over their heads (called, appropriately enough, "bucket baths"). The water can be heated on a stove prior to sudsing up. Others bring camping-style solar showers, which can serve as good, easy, and energy-efficient ways to enjoy a warm shower from time to time. (Though, in truth, they often go unused as volunteers acclimate to either warm bucket baths or cold showers.) In any case, you'll have the means to wash up and smell fresh on a regular basis.

16

Can I bring my pet overseas with me?

Unfortunately the Peace Corps does not allow volunteers to transport their pets to their overseas assignments. Though this policy may appear unduly stern, it exists for some good reasons. First, it wouldn't be any fun for the pet, especially during your three months of intensive on-site training. Besides the fact that you will be emotionally unstable, physically stressed, and extraordinarily busy, you'll probably also be stunned at how differently (and horribly) pets are treated in most developing countries.

In addition, handling the paperwork, legalities, quarantine requirements, and costs of transporting your pet overseas would entail an immense commitment of time and resources both here and overseas. With all that's required to prepare for your trip, the added burden of preparing your pet for the trip would complicate things exponentially. Once you arrive in-country, your schedule leaves no room for tending to the responsibilities associated with pet transfers.

The good news is that many PCVs adopt pets once they've settled into village life and feel more at home in the Peace Corps. Doing so usually saves a local animal from being abused (or even eaten) and provides an instant source of distraction, entertainment, and responsibility that makes the two years pass by a little easier. For more on adopting pets in the Peace Corps, refer to question 26.

Part III

Peace Corps Training— Learning the Ropes

17

What is training like?

Peace Corps training is an experience in and of itself. It is three months (give or take) of making new friends, taking new steps, learning about a different culture, and learning about yourself. It pampers you and challenges you, informs you and confuses you, allows you to grow but shelters you. Most importantly, it prepares you for two years on your own in an environment more foreign and exciting than any you've ever encountered.

The Peace Corps uses a methodology called "community-based training" (CBT) in a majority of the countries in which it operates now. CBT employs a decentralized approach whereby Peace Corps trainees (PCTs)—after an initial few days or weeks together for shots and group in-briefings on culture, safety, and other topics—are split up and placed into small communities or villages to live with home-stay families. From that point forward, training focuses on learning-by-doing in an immersion context, with guidance from qualified local Peace Corps trainers assigned to each village or volunteer cluster.

For many PCTs, the homestay experience itself is the most trying and rewarding part of the training program. As I mention above, soon after arriving in-country, you will be sent to live with a host family in a rural area for a portion or the entire length of the training program. Trainees are grouped in villages either by language ability or sector. Your host family may or may not speak English; they may be extremely poor, middle class, or relatively well off; and they may or may not have hosted a Peace Corps trainee before. The only thing you can be sure of is that they'll have a room for you and your belongings, and they will provide you with breakfast and possibly dinner, depending on their arrangements with the Peace Corps. They will be an excellent source of both cultural and linguistic immersion. You may really bond with them and keep in touch with them long after training is over; you may not. They may suffocate you, demanding to know where you are going at night and what time you'll be back for dinner (especially true for female trainees), or they may treat you like an adult, unconcerned with your schedule or your whereabouts. Meals prepared for you may be gastronomic delights or barely palatable local fare. They may have a TV, radio, toilet, shower, and telephone, or they may have a pit latrine and no electricity.

In my training group, we had all kinds of interesting homestay experiences. Some of us were really lucky and forged close, enduring relationships with our families; others had to switch to a different homestay family two or three times before settling in. Although most homestay experiences are positive or at least bearable, if you find that yours is intolerable (for instance, you're in an unreasonably dangerous part of town, your family fails to provide you with the agreed-upon meals, your room is a breeding ground for roaches and mosquitoes), ask for a transfer to a different family. You aren't stuck with the first family you get, and no one is expecting you to suffer through three months of hell in the name of cultural sensitivity.

Aside from the homestay experience, training is a rigorous and intensive few months of classes, seminars, field trips, projects, and evaluations. Once PCTs have moved in with their host families, language classes often comprise a big part of the morning and may be held in homestay houses or a nearby training center. Technical training and related activities follow in the afternoon: a trainee in the health sector may give hygiene presentations and build gardens, while education PCTs teach classes and water sanitation trainees construct latrines. The goal of this method is to integrate formal training with real-world practice at the local level, encouraging PCTs to gain confidence and self-reliance through a blend of managed course work and "learning through discovery."

Sandwiched into this strict timetable are weekly vaccinations, sessions on health and safety, cross-cultural and development seminars, and "homestay processing" (a forum to discuss your homestay experiences with other volunteers and trainers). In training, you work in groups and on individual projects, you are evaluated and make your own evaluations of your trainers, and you still find time to socialize and make friends.

Overall Peace Corps training focuses on the critical areas needed to nurture you from a clueless tourist to a seasoned veteran in a relatively short period of time. Despite the fact that you may at times feel a bit cloistered, it prepares you well for the difficult transition to life at post. Training is also an interesting experience in time management. The days are full, but so are the evenings and nights. After "formal" training, you still have to decide how to divvy up the remainder of the day. Do you stick around your homestay family's house to spend quality time bonding and playing with your little brothers and sisters? Do you meet up with fellow trainees to grab a bowl of beans and rice and a beer? Or do you go for a walk by yourself, seeking quiet time to think and process, absorb and evaluate? Somehow, over the three months of training, you'll find the time to do them all.

18
How hard will it be to learn the language? What language(s) will I learn?

The Peace Corps approach to language learning has been hailed as one of the best in the world. Rather than the conventional method of starting with vocabulary drills, verb conjugations, and personal pronoun memorization, trainees engage in direct dialogue with native speakers from day one. Before you know it, you're making connections and picking up vocab and tenses just by hearing them used correctly the first time around. The instructors are generally excellent, guiding you and correcting you, encouraging you and lauding your efforts regardless of your accent or speed. Every week or two you are reevaluated and placed in different groups depending on your progress. At the beginning of the day, you'll go around the room and answer basic questions like "How did you sleep?" and "Tell us something that you did last night with your homestay family." You'll get to hear how others answer and figure out ways to communicate your own thoughts so you are understood, even if you aren't "textbook" correct.

This conversational approach, learning by speaking and hearing, is punctuated with conventional lessons in grammar, tense, vocabulary, and conjugation—lessons that become enlightening interludes after struggling with sentences and wondering just how to say things like "I would have had" during the more interactive sessions of dialogue and exchange. At the end of twelve weeks, you will find yourself with a solid foundation from which to hone your foreign language skills over the next two years.

There are people who, no matter how hard they try, can't seem to progress at the rate required by the strict timetable of training.

For those people, language tutors and instructors are available for after-class sessions, lunchtime course work, and one-on-one training. Granted, it's no fun to grind through French or Spanish while your friends are throwing a Frisbee around or writing letters in the sun, but it's Peace Corps' way of telling you that they will not let you "fail" training so long as you have the interest and are willing to work with them.

As far as which languages you will learn, count on learning the national language first and foremost. Everyone will start out learning French, Spanish, Portuguese, Swahili, or whatever the official language may be. If your country has a predominant local language also spoken and used heavily, you'll probably be trained in that as well. Once you receive your post assignment, if there are a few weeks left in training, you may even start classes in small, local vernaculars spoken around the area where you'll be working. Peace Corps has the resources to teach you the language skills you need to function and work in your village. Take advantage of them to get a grip on the basics (at a minimum), then dive in headfirst to pick up the rest while you're out in the field.

There are often Peace Corps–sponsored language seminars offered at various points during your two years of service as well. Those classes are designed to gauge your progress, fine-tune your language skills, and get everyone together for some fun and relaxation. I'd advise keeping an ear open for opportunities like that; they help make it all come together and make you realize how far you've come at the same time.

19

Will I have enough technical training to do my job?

Eventually, yes. The Peace Corps' technical training program is a priority and is designed to provide everyone with a high level of competence. Although people from all levels of experience enter the program, each volunteer leaves training on fairly equal ground, equipped to do his or her job for two years independent of close supervision or scrutiny.

Your technical trainers will either be former Peace Corps volunteers who excelled in their jobs and have an enthusiasm for their work or contracted local experts who have been trained in Peace Corps' experiential learning methodologies and CBT program format. They will be excellent resources for gaining skills you'll need in the field and for providing nontechnical information about life in your country of service.

Technical training focuses on practical skills as opposed to theory or policy. If you're an agroforester, you'll spend the majority of your training time on a farm or demonstration plot getting your hands dirty. If you're a teacher, you'll spend lots of time in front of peers, students, and trainers honing your teaching skills. If you're a health worker, you'll practice giving presentations on health-related subjects in the local language. In many ways, once you reach your village, you'll feel as though you've already racked up substantive experience and won't be as intimidated as you initially anticipated.

Technical training starts with the basics, accommodating trainees who have minimal to no previous knowledge of the subject area. As with language training, if you start falling behind, you can get extra help and do additional work to catch up. You won't be trained in every aspect of your field, just in those aspects that allow you to accomplish programmatic work objectives. Peace Corps provides you with a foundation of knowledge during training to carry you through your first few weeks and months at post; from there it's your responsibility to supplement that training with hands-on, site-specific field experience.

At various points during your service, Peace Corps will host technical refresher courses called in-service training (IST). ISTs provide a chance to get out of your village, reconvene with other volunteers in your program, share ideas, and learn new techniques from your associate Peace Corps director (APCD) and guest speakers (often host country national professionals). ISTs can be useful in many ways. Beyond formal training planned for the week, you'll pick up important tips and pointers from more experienced volunteers who are nearing their close-of-service dates. Depending on how competent your APCD is, formal lectures and field demonstrations may shed light on problems or frustrations you have encountered at your work site. As with any Peace Corps gathering, ISTs also offer opportunities to socialize with friends and colleagues you may not have seen in a while.

Part IV

Managing Your Money

20
How will I get paid?
Where will I keep my money?

The Peace Corps pays its volunteers either monthly or quarterly, depending on where you serve. Once every pay period, the Peace Corps office in-country will make an electronic funds transfer directly to a locally contracted bank account. You will either have to go to the bank with your ID to withdraw your stipend over the counter or, depending on the bank and infrastructure in your area, you may be issued an ATM card that you can then use to access your funds just as you would in the States. Regardless of the setup in your country, bank fees often are very high, so volunteers generally minimize the number of transactions by withdrawing large amounts each time. If you happen to be posted to an area where banks lack electronic funds transfer capabilities, you may receive your stipend via check, which will be mailed to your local post office box by registered mail or deposited directly into the nearest bank by the Peace Corps.

In countries or villages where there are no stable banks to speak of, or the mail system is completely dysfunctional, someone from the office will travel to each region where volunteers are posted and distribute living allowances by hand (though this is a rarity nowadays). In other cases still, if you know you'll be coming into the Peace Corps office for medical or other purposes around the time that checks are being cut, you can have your administrative officer hold the check and pick it up yourself.

The way you store your money is up to you. If you have an account at an accessible, reputable, and reliable bank, you can keep it there. The bank may be in your town or village, or it may be in a nearby town which you visit every few weeks to stock up on supplies, visit other volunteers, and run errands. As long as you, other volunteers, and the Peace Corps administration have confidence in the bank and its operations, this option is generally the safest and easiest.

If you are wary of the banking system or are too far from a reputable bank to make practical use of it, you can withdraw your stipend every pay period and hide the money in your house. Keep in mind, however, the dangers involved in managing your money this way. House break-ins and Peace Corps robberies can be common, and if word gets around that a stash of money is hidden on the premises, you may find your house becoming an even bigger target than it already is. It may also be hard to budget yourself if your whole paycheck is available to you at all times. Volunteers who have to travel to a bank or some other secure location (such as the Peace Corps office) to withdraw funds usually stretch out their living allowances better than those who can dip into it at any time.

If you hide your money in your house, take extra care not to let anyone, including your best friend, trusted house help, neighbor, landlord, and the multitude of seemingly innocent kids who come around every day to play, see where your hiding place is. We had one instance in my program where a volunteer was spied taking money from her cache by the ten-year-old son of her neighbor. Though he never stole any of it, he disclosed the hiding place to his classmates and the following week almost $600 was missing.

If you are robbed, you can turn to the Peace Corps for "emergency funds" to carry you over until the next pay period. Sometimes, though, they may deduct those funds from future living allowance checks. They may also take it out of your readjustment allowance—money set aside for your completion of service, typically amounting to $225 for every month served, to use as you like. Regardless, you'll need to go to the Peace Corps office, file a theft report, and talk to your program director and administrative officer. The bottom line: Think carefully about how and where you keep your money and other valuables; you are already a target simply by virtue of the fact that you are a foreigner. Don't make the target bigger if you can help it.

21

Will I have enough money?
Should I bring extra money with me?

Yes, you will have enough money to live comfortably wherever you serve. By "comfortably," I mean you will have enough to eat balanced meals, go out for drinks, travel around, buy crafts and souvenirs, have clothes made, buy toiletries, give gifts and contributions at social functions, go to dinner and a movie when you're in the capital, and so on. Although the Peace Corps tries hard to promote a grassroots volunteer lifestyle and encourages you to "live at the level of your neighbors in the village," they have to balance that philosophy with the reality of keeping you healthy, happy, and productive. In other words, unless your neighbors are high-ranking government officials or successful businesspeople, you will generally be much better off than most of those around you at the village level.

Though I can't tell you exactly how much your living allowance will be, PCVs generally receive between $200 and $300 per month. These stipends vary based on local prices and inflation, volunteer feedback (from periodic surveys), and the Peace Corps' annual budget. Living allowances may also differ from region to region within a given country, reflecting relative price differences in basic commodities, housing, and so on. If local economic conditions deteriorate substantially during your service, your allowance may change while you are overseas to compensate. Suffice it to say, I knew of very few volunteers who found their allowances insufficient to cover their everyday costs in the Peace Corps. In the 2006 Volunteer Survey Report, most PCVs (81%) felt that their living allowance met their basic needs "adequately," "well," or "very well."

There may, however, be times when you find yourself short on cash due to events or expenses that are above and beyond your normal budget. Perhaps you take an extended vacation or purchase an expensive souvenir. In those instances, don't fret; you can always borrow from a fellow PCV, cash in a traveler's check or some American dollars if you brought some, or in real dire straits explain your situation to the Peace Corps administration to receive emergency funds or an advance on your next living allowance allotment. One way or another, you'll be covered.

The only other time during your service when you may not have enough money is during training. In training, since you aren't yet a volunteer, you receive a weekly stipend rather than the standard living allowance. As Peace Corps provides you with housing, meals, snacks, and a full schedule of classes and sessions to keep you busy, they don't anticipate that you'll need much spending money during training. You'll find, however, once you start exploring the area and discovering local bars, restaurants, and markets, you'll wish you had more than fourteen dollars per week in your pockets (that was the amount my training group received). For those initial months, I'd recommend bringing some American dollars or traveler's checks to exchange for local currency. Cash will always fetch you a better rate than checks, and there is no fee for changing cash, so bring bills—the bigger the better (currency exchange businesses often prefer to deal with fifty-dollar bills or higher). A couple hundred dollars provides a nice cushion, and, if you don't spend it during training, you'll appreciate the backup funds during lean months or special occasions that arise over the next two years.

Part V

Living Like the Locals

22

Will I live in a mud hut? Will I have electricity or running water?

These are typical questions that everyone who is thinking of joining the Peace Corps ponders. The answer is simple but a bit frustrating: it depends. Before I get into a discussion about why it depends, the following are some relevant statistics from the 2006 Peace Corps Volunteer Survey Report, produced by the Peace Corps Office of Planning, Policy, and Analysis (March 23, 2007):

Amenities:
- 75% of PCVs worldwide report having either a constant or fairly constant supply of electricity at their residences, compared with 18% who have no electricity at all.
- 62% of PCVs either always or usually have running water in their homes, compared with 26% who have none.
- Almost three-quarters (74%) of PCVs never have access to either email or the Internet at their residences, and 60% never have access at their work sites.
- Two-thirds (66%) lack access to a landline telephone at their residences, though over half (55%) have at least some access to a landline phone at their work sites.

Living arrangements:
- Most volunteers (72%) describe their sites as rural villages or towns (another 3% live on "outer islands").
- 60% do not live with a host country individual or family.
- PCVs in the business sector are more likely to live either in cities (31%) or country capitals (5%) than PCVs in other sectors.

- In addition, 72% of volunteers report that adequate housing was available immediately upon their arrival on-site, while another 19% found adequate housing within their first three months at post.

While the above statistics provide a good worldwide view, interpreting them gets a bit complex for prospective volunteers. Within the developing world, countries vary greatly in their level of development and the extent of their infrastructure. In Africa, for example, you'll find that some countries (Niger, Ethiopia, Malawi) are much less developed than others (South Africa, Botswana, Namibia). This disparity in economic wealth is reflected in the quantity and quality of their roads, telephone lines, network of electricity and running water, and construction of houses and buildings. If you are assigned to a country that has a relatively developed infrastructure, your chances of having running water and electricity in your village are greater than if you are sent to a severely depressed or less developed nation.

Your living conditions also depend on where you are posted within your country. You may find that there are certain regions that are better off than others. If you are assigned to a work site in a more developed area of your country (as business sector PCVs are), you may not only have paved roads, piped water, and electricity, but you may also have phone and Internet connectivity. Communities in the food-producing regions, the touristy spots, and the areas just outside of provincial capitals tend to be more modern than villages located in the heart of the undeveloped regions (rain forests, deserts, mountains).

Generally your program administrator will ask for your preferences regarding water/electricity/housing toward the end of training, before assigning you a post. This isn't to say your input will always be taken into consideration, but at least you'll have an opportunity to express your desires and hope for the best. Oftentimes a certain group of people will adamantly insist that they want a village without electricity or running water, while another group will prioritize those amenities, and almost everyone will end up getting what they want without competition.

I had both electricity and running water in my house, and though at times I felt like perhaps I wasn't getting the complete "bush experience," overall I realized that spending two years immersed in another country, language, and culture was, in many ways, exotic and challenging enough. In fact, I enjoyed using my portable stereo without buying cartons of batteries, washing my dishes and taking showers without hauling water from the stream, and reading at night to a light source that wasn't blackening my ceiling (and lungs) with kerosene smoke. Neither my electricity nor my taps were by any means reliable—they were out of service sporadically throughout my tour (sometimes for days, sometimes for weeks)—but their capricious quality only deepened my appreciation for them.

As for having your own house, most volunteers live by themselves for their two years overseas. If a house isn't set up and waiting when you arrive in your village, you may have to stay with a homestay family (identified by the Peace Corps in advance) while you look for houses available to rent. In some instances, you may need to have a house built for you, in which case you would stay with a family or colleague while it's being constructed. If there's a Peace Corps rest house nearby, you may be able to use it as a temporary base as well. In most cases, however, Peace Corps will have researched the housing situation in your local community well before your arrival and arranged with local leaders and counterparts to have something ready and waiting by the time you arrive.

Expenses associated with housing are covered by the Peace Corps, either as rent and utilities included in your living allowance or supplemental payment on an individual basis covering construction or remodeling costs (within reason). PCVs also receive a settling-in allowance when they move to their sites to cover the costs of purchasing basic supplies, furniture, linens, pots and pans, and so on.

If you prefer to stay with a homestay family in your village or live in a compound with your neighbors, you are welcome to do so. If you are posted to an extremely small village, for example, you may find it both impractical and culturally insensitive to live by yourself. Volunteers I knew who lived with families had rich and rewarding experiences, and often felt closer to the culture and society in which they served.

23

How will I wash my clothes?
Do my dishes? Clean my house?

If you're into it, do it yourself. If not, hire someone. Peace Corps volunteers routinely hire locals to clean, cook, and wash for them. Don't gasp—it's not as paternalistic or colonial as it may sound. It's offering someone in your village a job with wages that will pay their way through school or afford them the means of purchasing medicine for their children. In fact, when word gets out that you are in search of a house helper, there will be a line outside your door that winds around the village block.

Granted, not every volunteer hires a helper. I knew a few that were intent on washing every article of clothing, carrying every bucket of water, scrubbing every inch of floor space, and cooking every meal themselves for their entire two years. Of course, they were hounded regularly by kids, neighbors, acquaintances, and total strangers who were pleading for work and insisting that they could do a better job for a small salary. I do realize that some people just aren't comfortable with the idea of having a "maid" or "cook" care for them and their house—especially in the Peace Corps—but many volunteers think of it as an opportunity to provide an individual in the village with income, which is exactly what it is.

If you do decide to hire someone, there are a couple of arrangements you can make with that person. Many Peace Corps houses have annexes or back rooms in which a live-in housekeeper can stay, free of charge, on the condition that they do the agreed-upon chores and look after the house (and any pets) in the volunteer's absence. Oftentimes, if you have a live-in housekeeper, you'll end up forming a friendship with that person and his or her family that will quickly transcend the worker/supervisor relationship that first existed. On the other hand, there have been cases where live-in house help have robbed PCVs or taken advantage of the situation to violate the PCV's privacy in his or her absence. If you decide on the live-in arrangement, try to find someone who has worked with Peace Corps volunteers in the past (odds are they'll find you first, anyway), and don't be afraid to ask other volunteers in the area and friends of yours in the village about the applicant's character.

Other volunteers hire someone to come by once every week or two for a full day of sweeping, washing, dusting, and drying. That arrangement may be more convenient and sensible if you keep your house clean for the most part and only want help with the down-and-dirty scrubbing and washing. As with the live-in arrangement, check references and ask around before agreeing to hire someone to work for you on a part-time basis. Keep in mind, too, that in most villages in the developing world, there is no obsession with punctuality and scheduling as there is in America. If you've agreed with your house help to meet up in two weeks for another cleaning session, and the person shows up two hours late or not at all, there may be a myriad of reasons that are all perfectly acceptable and legitimate in that culture. So unless it gets out of hand, don't let it frustrate you. You'll find that to be true not just with your house help, but with your work in the Peace Corps in general.

24
What is the food like?

Local foods differ depending on the country, the region, and the local culture. Some volunteers, for example, are posted in areas where meat is abundant, but fruits and vegetables are scarce. For others, the opposite is true. Often you'll find familiar basic ingredients prepared in unfamiliar ways. Regardless of where you serve, however, be prepared to encounter new foods and dishes that may, at first, strike you as odd. Whether it's crocodile stew or fried grubs, you'll have the opportunity to find out just how different people's conceptions of food can be.

Aside from village fare, which may strike you as delicious, monotonous, or simply strange, you'll quickly discover the hot spots in bigger towns and the capital city where you can go once in a while for more familiar dishes—burgers, fries, pizzas, or banana splits. Don't count on frequenting those restaurants, as they are usually priced for tourists, expatriates, and wealthy HCNs, but take heart in knowing that every country has at least a few places where you'll be able to satisfy the occasional craving for comfort food and American cooking.

Though I can't tell you exactly what the food will be like in your area, if you keep an open mind and get excited to try new and different cuisines, you'll probably come back to the States two years down the road with cravings for that village dish that you can't find anywhere else in the world. If it turns out that you can't stand anything prepared locally, don't fret—as I mention in question 31, you'll have the means and time to create your own, more familiar dishes to get you through.

25

What if I'm a vegetarian?

True to the stereotype, many Peace Corps volunteers are vegetarian, and many who are not convert once they arrive overseas. You shouldn't have a problem preparing nutritious and balanced meals if you are a vegetarian, but you should pay careful attention to your protein intake. As I mention in question 29, most Peace Corps countries host a panoply of diseases that your body isn't accustomed to battling. Allowing yourself to become protein-deficient increases your vulnerability to those diseases. Most protein in developing countries comes from fish, meat, and/or beans. If you don't eat fish or meat, and you don't like beans, you may be in trouble. The Peace Corps has, in fact, designed a questionnaire just for vegetarian applicants, asking how you would react to various scenarios that could undermine your dietary habits, choices, and health (see appendix H).

In actuality, depending on where you serve, you may find a wide variety of farm-fresh vegetables and hand-picked fruits available at your local market. These foods are often grown organically, with no fertilizers or pesticides, and harvested within a day or two of the time you eat them. In the States, you'd pay premium prices at specialty grocery stores for the kinds of produce you'll find at some Peace Corps posts.

You may be wondering why meat eaters would be inclined to become vegetarian once they join the Peace Corps. In many cases, it's because they are posted to remote villages where the only meats available are taken from surrounding forests and savannah—animals like monkey, bat, and antelope—and they don't care for the taste or idea of eating them. In other cases, they visit the market in their villages and see the proverbial cow head and body parts hanging from hooks in the open air, flies and other bugs gorging freely. Others find that the price of meat in their village is exorbitant, perhaps because it is imported from faraway towns (probably transported in less than sterile conditions, to boot).

The only sticky situation you may encounter if you're a vegetarian in the Peace Corps is the occasional meal at a friend's or colleague's house where meat is bought, prepared, and offered to you as a gesture of hospitality. In those instances, it can be incredibly awkward to explain that you don't eat meat for moral, health, or taste reasons. Your hosts will have spent precious money on the meat and will probably have placed the best portion on your plate. Vegetarian friends of mine who found themselves in those situations usually bit the bullet and ate. Others proffered religious excuses ("I am sorry, but my religion forbids me from eating meat. I deeply appreciate the trouble you have gone through to make me feel welcome") to get out of the predicament—the only excuse that may actually work.

It's worth noting that, in some countries and regions, vegetarian PCVs have been known to forgo their habitual diets and start eating meat again. In Eastern Europe and parts of sub-Saharan Africa, meat dishes are prepared so well and are so enticing, even stalwart vegetarians occasionally throw in the flag. Fruits and vegetables in those areas are often too scarce or too costly to serve as the basis for balanced and nutritious meals, compounding the pressure to eat meat. But don't let that scare you. Committed and resourceful vegetarians, no matter where they are posted, can usually find ways to stick to their diets if they wish.

26

Can I buy or adopt a pet overseas?

Absolutely. In fact, Peace Corps pets are a valuable and integral part of the experience for many volunteers. They keep you company, they keep you busy, and they usually keep you a bit safer at post. If you get a cat, it will chase away mice and rid your house of roaches and spiders. If you get a dog, it will alert you to visitors and guard your house when you are away. Some volunteers get so attached to their pets, they bring them back to the States after their service is over (see question 73).

I had a cat, and though I've never considered myself to be much of a "cat person," I can't imagine having gone through my two years without her. She was affectionate and playful, and was an adept mouser. I found that having a cat was practical for many reasons. She definitely provided me with constant company, but she was also easy to feed and clean. When I left, I passed her on to my replacement and, last I heard, she's healthy and happy and continuing to supply volunteers with new kittens.

A good number of Peace Corps volunteers have dogs—village pups that they acquire as gifts from neighbors or colleagues. Dogs are great Peace Corps pets but are higher maintenance. They tend to get dirtier, cause more trouble (chasing local goats, chickens, and kids), require more training, and need more attention than cats. Plus, dogs need babysitters when you leave your post for extended periods, whereas cats are virtually self-sufficient.

The upside of having a dog, as any dog lover will tell you, is that they shower more unconditional love on you and can provide you with more company than some of your best human friends. They may also serve as better security guards than your neighbors or house help. As I mentioned above, most volunteers in my area who had dogs became so attached to them they considered bringing them back to the States. The same wasn't true for those with pet cats.

27

How will my neighbors and colleagues view me?

This depends, in large part, on where you serve. In general, however, you'll find that Peace Corps' reputation as an effective, motivated, committed, and dynamic development organization is unsurpassed. The longer Peace Corps has served in a particular country, the more widespread and positive its reputation. Since volunteers serve at the grassroots level, while Peace Corps administration works directly with government officials, rich politicians and poor farmers alike become familiar with the organization. As a result, volunteers are often welcomed by their counterparts and neighbors, and are treated with respect by those they encounter wherever they venture during their two years overseas.

Of course, there are occasions when Peace Corps' reputation seems a bit less inviolate. Some government officials may perceive Peace Corps volunteers as obtrusive foreigners who flaunt their immunity to local customs (translated: refuse to pay bribes during certain transactions). There are parts of the world—particularly those with a history of U.S. influence in national politics—where volunteers are presumed to be covert intelligence operatives and hence are viewed with great suspicion. Some villagers and local townspeople may regard volunteers as spoiled Americans with misplaced values—rich enough to forsake high-paying job opportunities in the States and callous enough to abandon their families for two years. Others may have been exposed to PCVs in social scenes and reached the conclusion that volunteers are nothing more than drunken socialites. But those "bad raps" are few and far between in comparison to the impression of PCVs as devoted, culturally sensitive, and uniquely giving members of the development community. With that in mind, your job will be easier if you do your part to uphold the positive aspects of Peace Corps' reputation or establish it if it hasn't already been established in your village.

What you may find surprising, regardless of where you serve, is the degree to which American culture has invaded the developing world. From the highlands of Nepal to the deserts of sub-Saharan Africa, you'll find counterfeit Nike sportswear, bootlegged American music and movies, blue jeans, Coca-Cola, and other random fragments of Americana on proud display in local shops and markets. Without a deeper understanding of this country and all its intricacies, many people in the developing world infer from those images that all Americans are rich, powerful, socially aggressive people. Even if your neighbors and colleagues have no clue about the Peace Corps, when they discover you are an American, they will make assumptions about you based on the stereotypes that are gift-wrapped and exported by our pop culture. Though the assumptions may be laughably inaccurate, in most cases they'll be harmless and entertaining foundations from which you can educate the people who judge you by them.

28

How will I travel around my work area?

It used to be that every Peace Corps volunteer (or nearly every one) was issued a motorcycle after training as a means of traveling to work sites and maximizing work productivity and efficiency. Then someone compiled statistics on the leading causes of Peace Corps deaths and discovered that the number one killer of PCVs was, lo and behold, motorcycle accidents. Everything from drunken riding to hitting a coconut at thirty miles per hour on a dirt road was to blame. So began the moto phaseout, which has by and large been completed.

Although it would be a rarity to be issued your own motorcycle these days, the use of "moto-taxis" in many countries (hailing a passing motorcycle and catching a ride for a few cents) is commonplace. Rules governing motorcycle use—even as a passenger—are determined by country directors, and thus vary greatly from post to post. For those who condone the use of moto-taxis, helmets are often mandatory, meaning that if you're caught riding without one, you can be reprimanded or even administratively separated from PC service.

More than likely, if you are assigned to a program or area that requires travel to various work sites and villages, you will be issued a mountain bike. Initially Peace Corps gave volunteers forty-pound Huffys with no tools. Today volunteers can look forward to receiving a relatively new (maybe second or thirdhand) midlevel Trek or something similar. You'll get a complete set of tools, a saddle bag, a pump, a water bottle, a helmet, a front and rear light, extra parts, and a manual on how to fix and maintain your bike. You'll also attend a mandatory two- to three-day bike class to learn the basics of assembly, maintenance, and riding.

Aside from the obvious exercise and health benefits, odds are you'll be the only person in your village with such a funky-looking bike, able to climb steep and rutted hills and descend faster than your average goat. It'll be a conversation piece and a head-turner. It'll get you in good with the kids in your village (who will stand and stare at it for hours while you're teaching your class or working your farms) and will provoke smiles, nods, and thumbs-up signs as you cruise through the center of town on your way back home. Also, most Peace Corps posts offer excellent mountain-bike riding opportunities—single-track galore and dirt roads everywhere. People in the States drive for hours with their bikes on top of their cars to find terrain like that!

In addition to bikes, some Peace Corps countries may provide funding for volunteers to purchase truly indigenous means of transportation including horses, donkeys, or camels. One RPCV familiar with the difficulties of "horse upkeep" in the Dominican Republic, however, advises that such requests be thought through carefully before moving forward. Galloping to your work site astride a saddle may seem much easier than pedaling up a mountainside, but bikes don't require food, water, medicine, or room to roam while parked.

Although most Peace Corps countries issue or allow for some form of transportation for their volunteers, there are those that encourage you to let your feet do the walking. Reasons include terrain, location of posts, program requirements, and so on. Once you find out where you are going, call Peace Corps or read through the materials they send you to see what they say on this topic. In Cameroon, agro-forestry, aquaculture, health, and community development volunteers had bikes (and, in the distant past, motorcycles). Education volunteers (both TEFL and math/science) didn't get anything because it was expected that they would live close to their schools, obviating the need for an improved means of reaching their work sites or covering more territory. Certain education volunteers who really wanted bikes, however, successfully petitioned their program directors and requisitioned those old forty-pound Huffys that were lying around the office—so there is hope!

Part VI

Common Medical and Safety Concerns

29
Will I get sick?

Yes, you will get sick. As with my response to "Will I be lonely?" irrespective of where you are or what you're doing in any given two-year period, you are guaranteed to get sick at least a few times. The difference, and the real worry, is whether or not you'll be sick for the whole two years (or for a good part of it). Being in a developing country often means exposing yourself to a host of weird diseases, parasites, and ailments, which can be very discouraging for someone who otherwise really wants to join the Peace Corps—not to mention the ways it can affect your family's support of your decision to join the Peace Corps.

The reality is, you will be inoculated against lots of terrifying diseases. You will receive extensive training on how to avoid contracting everything from filaria to malaria. You will, at first, be adamant about staying clean and healthy, determined to defy the odds. Then you'll come down with something—maybe amoebas, maybe bacterial dysentery, maybe scabies, or something as benign as a chigger (a mite that causes itching). At that point, the first step on your path toward a more relaxed (and realistic) outlook on getting sick will be taken. Over time, you'll realize how pointless it is to be paranoid about everything you touch and eat. You'll also realize that, using common sense, it is possible to minimize the risks to your health. Then you'll relax and spend two years marveling at the ways your body handles some pretty strange things.

I was one of the most anal volunteers around when it came to hygiene and attempts to ward off the diseases that commonly afflicted my fellow PCVs. I washed my hands before every meal, I let my clothes dry for three days before wearing them (to kill any mango-fly eggs), I boiled and filtered my water, I took my malaria prophylaxis religiously, I soaked my veggies in iodine before eating them, and so on. Yet, within my two years, I still managed to get giardiasis, bacterial dysentery, amoebas, malaria, chiggers, tumbo worms, fevers, diarrhea, and strange bites, marks, scratches, and rashes that came and went with the winds. I'm not trying to scare you; I only wish to convey to you how common, bearable, and in many ways unavoidable getting sick in the Peace Corps is. In fact, PCVs often perceive illnesses as more of an inconvenience and a hot topic of conversation than anything else.

Regardless of your tolerance level for illness or disease, you should be sure to report any persistent or truly unusual conditions to the Peace Corps Medical Officer (PCMO), just in case they become chronic. This is not only important for the sake of bureaucracy and documentation, but is a potential liability consideration as well. Treatment for longer-term ailments contracted during your service, if on file, may be eligible for coverage after you return to the States. Depending on what you come down with, this could be an important benefit.

Suffice it to say, you will not be sick every day for two years, nor will you look back when you COS and think, "If it weren't for all those diseases, I would have had a great experience." More than likely, you'll come to accept various medical problems as part of life in the Peace Corps. You shouldn't let your guard down when it comes to hygiene and health care, right up until your last day in-country, but you shouldn't fret now over what may happen later. When you do get sick overseas, you'll see that it isn't the end of the world, and it certainly isn't the end of your Peace Corps service . . . or at least it needn't be.

30
Will I get worms?

I stuck this question in only because, upon returning to the States, so many people asked me if I had worms while I was in the Peace Corps. Plenty of prospective volunteers have also expressed a wary, inquisitive fascination with the topic. Proud tales of surviving intestinal parasites are plentiful in many Peace Corps countries, but not all. Your odds of getting worms are dependent, in large part, on where you are posted. In Africa, South and Central America, and Asia, you may get a worm or two during your service. I managed to get through my two years worm-free, but plenty of my fellow PCVs had their day in the sun with lab results in hand and a look of horror on their face. For those who are considering joining the Peace Corps but are particularly worried about (and discouraged by the thought of) getting worms, take heart in the fact that there are plenty of commonsense things you can do to protect yourself from ever having to deal with this.

Here are some quick-and-easy tidbits to keep in mind while you're over there: Be sure to wash your hands each and every time before you eat. The most common way to get stomach worms is to have dirt under your fingernails. That dirt can harbor worm larvae invisible to the eye. If you don't wash your hands and keep your nails trimmed, you can easily ingest the larvae as you eat, and they'll gestate in your belly. Also, wash and soak in iodine any fresh fruits and vegetables you don't intend to cook before eating.

If you do get worms, don't panic. There are various kinds of worms out there, but most can be taken care of with a few pills. You may suspect you have worms if you notice a prolonged change in appetite, loss of energy, problems with bowel movements, gas, and so on. All you'll need to do is visit the Peace Corps medical office; they'll run the required tests and prescribe the appropriate medicine.

Consider it another character-building life experience to brag about when you get home.

If you find yourself overly paranoid about (or sickly fascinated with) the thought of getting worms, don't worry about it—this whole topic will be dealt with thoroughly in your three months of in-country training. As I mentioned, there are things you can do to minimize your chances of getting worms. Many volunteers successfully complete their service without playing host to an uninvited invertebrate. If you do get them, as with most other ailments common in the Peace Corps, it won't be as big a deal as you think it will be. I promise.

31
Will I lose weight? Gain weight?

If you ask this question of returned volunteers, you'll probably hear the same thing no matter where they served—everyone seems to put on a few pounds during the initial three months of training, then the "Peace Corps diet" kicks in and many people shed pounds once they settle into life at post. Training is a time when you'll be grouped with fellow recruits, eating shared meals that are almost always prepared for you, and following a daily routine that will be more mentally than physically exhausting. Once you get to your host community, however, the rigors of daily life combined with the demands of self-sufficiency generally result in some degree of weight loss.

Regardless of small fluctuations, the important thing is to be mindful of your diet and to keep it balanced whenever possible. Virtually every Peace Corps post around the world will have basic ingredients available for preparing healthy meals. Many of these ingredients will be grown and sold locally, others (such as dairy products, prepackaged foods, certain spices, and so on) might only be available in the nearest big town for a price that may seem relatively expensive on a Peace Corps budget. Just remember that without your health, it will be hard to enjoy any of your Peace Corps experience, so splurge and stock up.

It goes without saying that the most control you'll have over your diet will be the meals you cook at home. Eating out is great once in a while, especially if the local fare is tasty (which it often is). But if you don't already know how to cook, pay attention when you get together with more culinarily inclined volunteers and watch how they prepare spaghetti sauces, fajitas, and vegetable stews. You may not leave Peace Corps with gourmet cooking skills, but you can leave with a talent for making good, healthy meals out of raw ingredients and basic spices.

32

What medical services will be available to me?

This is an important question, and one that most prospective volunteers and their families want answered clearly. As you can imagine, the Peace Corps isn't interested in sending healthy volunteers overseas, only to have them return with debilitating illnesses or injuries. Instead they have a four-tiered system for ensuring that all volunteers are placed in safe environments and given adequate medical training and services.

First, the Peace Corps screens all applicants to identify any pre-existing medical conditions or requirements that either preclude them from joining or necessitate special placement (see appendix D). If, for example, you have an allergy to the drugs used to treat malaria, you may be disqualified from serving in Africa and be sent someplace in Eastern Europe or Central Asia instead. This minimizes the chances that you'll aggravate an existing or known potential health problem while you're overseas.

Second, the Peace Corps hires certified doctors, nurses, nurse practitioners, and physicians' assistants to staff their field offices. This means that, in every country Peace Corps serves, there will be at least one of the above-mentioned medical personnel stationed at the Peace Corps office whose sole job is to tend to the medical needs of volunteers. There may also be a roving area Peace Corps medical officer, based out of a centrally located Peace Corps office, who travels to a number of countries in the region to offer specialized services and medical care.

To be perfectly frank, you'll hear from some RPCVs that the quality of services provided by these Peace Corps doctors and nurses around the world is questionable. In fact, there are more than a few horror stories that portray the Peace Corps' medical field staff as incompetent or inexperienced. Unfortunately some of the stories are true. But to the organization's credit, medical personnel are always available to address your health and safety concerns in-country and to ensure that you receive treatment when necessary.

The third tier of the Peace Corps' medical program is integrated into the volunteer training curriculum. During your three months of training, you'll spend a few hours each week learning ways to avoid contracting all kinds of diseases, parasites, and illnesses. You'll learn how to properly prepare your food and water, how to maintain good hygiene, and how to ensure personal safety at all times. You will be made aware of the gamut of possible ailments that can affect you, and you will be told how to treat those ailments yourself, when possible. At the end of the training program, you will be issued a medical kit ("med kit"), containing a first aid manual, various over-the-counter drugs (aspirin, cortisone, Bacitracin, Tums, Sudafed, and so on), bandages, syringes, and the like. If you are in a malaria-endemic country, you'll be given prophylaxes (mefloquine, doxycycline, chloroquine, palludrine, perhaps Malarone) and curatives (Fansidar). You'll also be given a bountiful supply of condoms—enough to build your own raft and sail around the world with. In addition, you may receive the book *Where There Is No Doctor*, an illustrated owner's manual for the human body.

The fourth and last tier is referred to in Peace Corps jargon as "medivac." It stands for medical evacuation—a procedure for dealing with PCVs whose illnesses or injuries cannot be reasonably treated in-country. Medivacked volunteers are flown to the nearest country where adequate medical services and equipment exist. Often that country ends up being the United States, in which case the volunteer is sent directly to Washington, D.C.

If you are medivacked, the Peace Corps medical staff in Washington will review your file to determine when, if at all, you may return to your country of service. The quicker your recovery time, the better your odds of picking up where you left off. In some instances, you may be presented with the choice of returning to your post or resigning from the Peace Corps (called "medically separated" by the Peace Corps administration). In others, you may automatically be medically separated by the Peace Corps' Office of Medical Services, based on their determination of your condition (though you can appeal to the medical director in Washington, D.C.). An example of the latter would be a knee injury that requires reconstructive surgery and nine months of intensive rehabilitation. Again, much depends on the reasons for your medivac and the time frame for your recovery.

33

What if I become too sick to reach help?

This is a question that beleaguers many prospective volunteers and stirs fear in the hearts of their families. What if, one fateful day in your village, you are struck with some loathsome, mortal disease and impaired to the point where you can't even cry for assistance, let alone get treatment? What if you fall so ill, you can't endure the nine-hour donkey ride to civilization and you die a lonely death in the middle of nowhere?

For discussions on getting sick and using the Peace Corps' medical services, see question 32. In truth, most PCVs experience little or no difficulty getting treatment when they need it. In the extremely rare instance when a volunteer is too sick to seek help, and the medicines in the Peace Corps' med kit aren't effective, that individual will be transported to a local hospital or clinic by friends or neighbors. From there, the Peace Corps medical office will be contacted. I can think of no realistic combination of circumstances that would result in a volunteer falling sick and suffering alone in his or her village, untreated for a long enough period to have something life-threatening occur. One way or another, that person would administer self-treatment, be treated locally, transport him- or herself to the PC clinic, or be transported to a clinic by other volunteers or local friends.

Keep in mind that, in the Peace Corps, you are far from inconspicuous. If you go even a day without speaking to neighbors or being seen in the market, people start to wonder and worry. Friends and colleagues will always stop by your house to greet you and bring gifts— even after you've been in the village for a year. You will also be familiar enough with the local communications network to know how to reach someone in case of an emergency. Living in a fishbowl has its disadvantages, but being isolated in a time of need is not one of them.

34

What if I get pregnant or impregnate someone while I'm in the Peace Corps?

More volunteers than you might think have had to deal with this issue at some point during their service. The procedure varies, depending on the circumstances. Only a few constants apply, which are (1) the Peace Corps medical officer and country director must be notified once the pregnancy is discovered, and (2) if it's the volunteer who is pregnant, she will not be allowed to continue her service unless PC grants approval based on both medical and programmatic considerations.

That said, here are a few scenarios and the Peace Corps' policies for dealing with them:

A. A female volunteer gets pregnant and decides to have an abortion:

The volunteer is counseled, then medivacked home to have the abortion and may return to her country of service once she has recovered (with permission from the Peace Corps medical office in Washington, D.C.). Although the procedure itself is not paid for by the Peace Corps, medical complications that may arise from the procedure are covered. With abortions, it's two strikes and you're out, so a second request would be grounds for permanent medical separation.

B. A female volunteer gets pregnant and decides to carry the pregnancy to term:

1. If she decides to deliver the child in the States, she is medivacked there at Peace Corps' expense, where she remains under PC care and allowances for up to forty-five days. After that—unless

authorized to return to post with the newborn child (extremely rare)—she is medically separated from the Peace Corps.

2. If she decides to give birth in-country (not a common scenario, but perhaps the dad is a host country national and the Peace Corps has determined that local medical facilities meet certain standards), she may seek the country director's approval for continued service after delivery of the child. This would, in the unlikely event that it were approved, entitle her to maternity leave, child care, health care, and documentation services for the newborn. A more common scenario is that the volunteer is "field separated," meaning her contract with the Peace Corps is terminated, but she is allowed to continue living abroad if she wishes.

C. A male volunteer impregnates a host country national and acknowledges paternal ties:

The Peace Corps encourages the volunteer to provide support to the mother and child as part of his paternal responsibilities. The volunteer may be administratively separated, however, if his ability to fulfill his work requirements is hindered or if the Peace Corps' credibility is diminished by the incident. The same is true if the volunteer has violated host country laws or customs by impregnating the HCN.

D. A male volunteer impregnates a host country national but doesn't acknowledge paternal ties:

The Peace Corps does not get involved unless, as mentioned above, the volunteer's ability to work and maintain his program's credibility are adversely affected, in which case he may be administratively separated.

Under "extenuating circumstances," the above policies may not apply or may be modified on a case-by-case basis, but what I have outlined is what one can normally expect in those scenarios. My advice—make use of the Peace Corps' free condoms and avoid the scene altogether.

35

Is AIDS a big concern for Peace Corps volunteers?

This is a heavy topic, and one that is dealt with thoroughly during training and subsequent IST. According to United Nations statistics from 2004, over 96 percent of new HIV infections occur in the developing world—precisely the areas in which PCVs work and live for two years or more. Soon after you arrive in-country, you'll be shown a video featuring interviews with five returned volunteers who contracted the AIDS virus while serving overseas. All of them were infected by host country nationals. Several of them had their partners tested and were tested themselves at the Peace Corps medical office at some point during their two years. In each of those cases, the tests came back negative, which the volunteers took as license to abandon the use of contraceptives (condoms). But, as it turned out, either the tests failed to account for the "six-month window" or their partners were unfaithful after they were tested. In any case, they all had AIDS and the video serves as an effective eye-opener.

The medical office will literally shower you with condoms during your service. Trojans are stuffed into your med kit and are available by the handful at the office. In many countries, condoms can be bought locally too. If you decide to engage in sexual activities with a host country national, the office recommends having him or her tested and being adamant about using contraceptives even if you both are HIV negative. The same is true if you decide to engage in sexual activities with other PCVs, but since the AIDS rate is often exponentially higher in developing countries, the risks can be greater if you're with a host country national.

If you are infected with HIV, you will be medivacked for counseling and treatment in D.C. My advice to you is simply this: be extra careful, and extra aware, of all STDs while you are a volunteer. There may be times when you are lonely, drunk, romanced, pressured into compromising situations, or all of the above simultaneously. Don't ever let your guard down, and don't ever assume that your partner is "safe." The means to protect yourself will be everywhere—use them and avoid turning a two-year experience into a lifetime's sacrifice.

36

What if there is a crisis and I have to be evacuated from my post?

Peace Corps evacuations are very real occurrences, planned for by the zworld are more prone to events leading to evacuations than others. Political instability, civil unrest, military coups, election turmoil, media crackdowns, economic crises, territorial disputes, cultural clashes, and a host of other problems can, independently or combined, erupt into violence and threaten the security of Peace Corps volunteers working in affected areas. Although the Peace Corps generally tries to limit its programs to countries that are socially, politically, and economically stable, often such occurrences arise without much warning and escalate rather quickly.

If you are unfortunate enough to get caught up in a situation that requires emergency action, you will receive instructions from the Peace Corps via communication channels established when you first arrive at your post. For this reason, it is important to keep Peace Corps informed of your whereabouts if you plan to travel away from your assigned location for any substantive length of time. Instructions may range from self-imposed "house arrest" (sit tight until things cool down) to evacuation from your country of service. In the event that you are evacuated, the Peace Corps will arrange for your transportation to the capital city, if necessary.

I witnessed only one evacuation while I was in the Peace Corps, which occurred when civil war threatened volunteers in a neighboring country. PCVs were evacuated to Cameroon, where they stayed until the Peace Corps decided on an appropriate next step. Some ended up transferring into my program and serving their remaining time in Cameroon; others opted to COS and return to the States. No one was harmed during the evacuation, but all were affected by the violence and destruction they had witnessed before leaving. Fortunately, as I mentioned above, such occurrences are rare.

37

Do local police and government officials harass volunteers?

As with so many other aspects of Peace Corps life, it depends. In my village and region, police and "gendarmes" (army personnel) generally respected the Peace Corps but were known to hassle volunteers traveling without their Peace Corps ID. In other countries, however, volunteers seldom have run-ins with the police or government soldiers and the encounters that they do have are cordial and friendly. Looking at the PCV world collectively, only 6 percent of volunteers reported in a 2006 Volunteer Survey that they often or always felt threatened during police stops when traveling, versus 69 percent who said they never did.

If you happen to be assigned to a country where local and national police have been known to harass volunteers or detain them in the hopes of procuring bribes, you'll be instructed during training on various ways to deal with the situation, and you'll be told who to turn to in the event that the situation gets ugly. In most cases, deferring to authority is usually a placating and effective strategy for bowing out of potentially confrontational situations. Other times, you may have to throw your weight around and threaten "embassy" or "headquarters" involvement if things feel like they are getting out of hand.

In most cases, officials who harass Peace Corps volunteers are looking for a bribe from the "rich Americans." If you speak a local language or can effectively explain what you are doing in the country, all the while refusing to provide a payoff and insisting that you are as poor as your neighbors, odds are they'll tire and eventually let you go. What I don't recommend is offering a bribe or paying an official if he threatens to jail you for whatever reason. Doing so sets a dangerous precedent for yourself and future volunteers by raising the hopes and expectations of corrupt officers, who may begin to see Peace Corps volunteers as ready sources of supplements to their incomes.

38

Is sexual harassment a problem for female volunteers?

Unfortunately it can be. Over 45 percent of women in the Peace Corps experience some form of sexual harassment during the course of a year in their host countries (2006 Volunteer Survey). Although 94 percent of the cases are verbal rather than physical, this number is disturbingly high and is the topic of several reports issued by the Peace Corps each year, including the Office of Safety and Security's "Safety of the Volunteer Report" (viewable on the www.peacecorps.gov website).

Women in most developing countries do not enjoy as much freedom, respect, or authority as women in developed countries do. They are often deprived of economic and political power, and denied rights that women in the West view as elementary. Conversely, in many developing countries, men dominate the power structure of state, business, community, and home. As such, female volunteers may be perceived and treated differently than their male counterparts by host country nationals. The export of U.S. pop culture—romance novels, MTV, fashion magazines, and so on—compounds the problem by portraying American women as promiscuous and sexually permissive. In Cameroon, French-dubbed American soap operas were a big hit via satellite television, as were sexually explicit Western films and pop icons/sex symbols.

In general, the Peace Corps insists that volunteers be sensitive to the "effect their behavior has on their personal safety." They also maintain that the Peace Corps experience almost always requires volunteers to "adopt lifestyles sensitive to host country cultural norms" (Peace Corps Volunteer Manual, MS204: Section 3.1). Despite volunteers' best efforts to minimize exposure to sexual harassment, however, situations may arise for which deference and sensitivity are decidedly inadequate responses. If you are verbally harassed and you feel the attack is not rooted in cultural misunderstanding, by all means express your intolerance and proactively assert yourself. The prerogative is always yours to speak up when you feel harassed; you are only encouraged by the Peace Corps to think twice, since so many conflicts stem from misinterpretations and cultural differences.

Unwanted physical contact or sexual assault is another story. There is no instance when such behavior is justified, regardless of cultural divergences. In some countries, the Peace Corps encourages female volunteers to be aggressive and fight back when sexually assaulted, since a woman resisting a man is so uncommon it takes the aggressor by surprise. Many women PCVs carry pepper spray, whistles, or other items to alarm or disarm assailants. These items are sometimes provided by Peace Corps or the Regional Security Office of the American embassies overseas. In Cameroon, the Peace Corps sponsored a two-day training course to teach all PCVs the basics of self-defense. Depending on where you serve, your Peace Corps training program may spend a considerable amount of time preparing volunteers to handle sexual harassment in the field.

If your physical security is ever threatened during your service, immediately inform your program and country directors. If the situation doesn't improve with time, most requests for transfer to a different post are granted. In rare instances when volunteers are grievously assaulted, they are evacuated to the States for medical treatment and counseling.

As in the United States, your best weapons are awareness and preparedness. When overseas, use common sense and heed the Peace Corps' advice on the subject, which will be tailored to your country of service. Don't compromise your values or safety, but realize that life in the Peace Corps may require a respect for cultural differences that may, at times, infuriate you. Most importantly, should you ever personally experience sexual assault or intolerable harassment, remember that you have the right to respond, react, and report the incident just as you would in the States.

Part VII

Staying in Touch with Home

39

How will I receive mail
in the Peace Corps?

Most Peace Corps posts are in remote locations in impoverished countries where the mail system is often rudimentary, unreliable, and anything but private. When you are halfway across the world, however, such a system somehow seems adequate. In the Peace Corps, even a three-month-old letter seems like a blessing, and a package that arrives with only half the contents pilfered by customs officials is like a Christmas gift from Santa himself.

That said, there are a few things you can do to help hasten and secure the passage and delivery of your mail. Have anyone sending you a care package scribble religious symbols and biblical quotes all over the outside of the box. This sounds silly, but it works. Along every step of the way, your mail will be subject to the whims of postal officials, customs officers, and delivery personnel who often take the liberty of rummaging through care packages in search of goodies from the States. If your mail is embellished with religious symbols, the odds of keeping it intact are improved. You may even want to ask the sender to write "Sister" or "Brother" before your name, to heighten the effect.

Another trick is to have your mail addressed to you in red ink. I've been told red ink is somewhat sacrosanct in many third world societies and is reserved for only the most official of letters and correspondences. Though I'm unsure about this explanation's validity, I can vouch for the trick's effectiveness, having seen several packages addressed in red ink delivered safely and expeditiously.

Before you leave the States, find out from the Peace Corps the address of your training site. That is where you'll be for your first three months overseas, so I recommend having friends and family start writing weeks before you leave the States if you want to get mail soon after you arrive. I didn't do that and consequently suffered through a grueling six-week period of mail silence before letters started trickling in. Once you know your village assignment, get a P.O. box at the closest post office as soon as possible. If you're posted to a bigger village or town, there may be a post office within walking distance of your house. If you're in a more remote location, you may have to take a bush taxi to the nearest big town to check your mail.

There is often an informal and effective system in the Peace Corps of having neighboring volunteers, who pass by or through your village, deliver mail to you on their way back from a mail run. Sometimes, if there is a cluster of volunteers who all get mail in the provincial capital or nearest big town, they will rent a P.O. box together and have copies of the key made. Other times there may be a Peace Corps rest house set up in a centrally located town, and any mail picked up from the local post office will get distributed to individual boxes in the Peace Corps house.

Picking up packages is a bit more complicated and can often turn into an entire afternoon's affair. You may receive a note from the post office declaring that they are in custody of a package addressed to you and indicating the official taxes and tariffs due to post bail and claim it. Notice I said "official." What they will not inscribe on the postal slip are the numerous unofficial bribes and gifts expected when you show up with your imploring look and desperate smile. They may double the declared fee; they may have you open your box in front of them and demand some of the contents (such as food items or magazines). I recommend that you stand firm and offer them nothing. Don't pay any bribes; don't give any gifts. It sets a bad precedent. If you loiter around and whine about the evils of corruption long enough, they'll tire of you and relinquish your package just to get you to leave. It should be noted that some PCVs, particularly those with access to small, rural post offices, genuinely bond with postal workers and share incoming goodies with them to be friendly. This, however, is the exception rather than the rule.

Sending packages back home can also be tricky. Don't send items of value from your country of service to the States unless volunteers who have been there for a while have tried it and declared it to be safe. One PCV in my group insisted on sending all his film back home to be developed rather than developing it in-country. He once sent a batch of five rolls, documenting his first three months at post, to his parents. They never received them, and he was devastated. Not every package you send from your country of service will disappear in transit. It will depend on where you serve and what you are sending (to a degree). But if you are burned even once, it will feel like once too many.

A surprising number of countries scattered throughout the developing world do have UPS offices in the larger cities. Though they will be reliable and insurable sources of mail transport, the cost of sending something back to the States via UPS is usually prohibitively high for Peace Corps volunteers.

Aside from packages, sending letters is relatively simple. No matter where you are, you should be able to get your hands on aerograms—that waxy, tissue-thin blue stationery that costs almost nothing to send, and allows you to squeeze in a couple of pages of text if you write small. Aerograms almost always find their way to their destination; it's just a question of how many detours and delays they encounter en route.

One sure way of transporting letters and packages both to and from the States is to have guests visiting Peace Corps volunteers act as couriers. If one of your fellow PCVs is expecting a visitor from the States, ask if you can arrange to have your family mail the visitor a letter or small package to be hand delivered to you. This assures quick and safe delivery. When that visitor is heading back to the States, ask if he or she minds carrying a few letters or a small preaddressed and prestamped package to send to your friends or family. Burdensome as it may seem, you will assuredly be called on to return the favor one day when you have visitors from the States, so don't be shy.

Finally, if you absolutely need something sent to you and wish to maximize the chances of it arriving in one piece, have it sent to the Peace Corps office rather than to your village or local post office. Eliminating the additional transport and handling required to deliver the package closer to you reduces the odds that an intermediary will steal it. The Peace Corps office is also a more "official" destination than your local post office, making it a less likely target for foul play. Once the office receives it, they'll send a note to your local P.O. box and you can pick it up the next time you're in town.

40

Will people be able to send me things through the embassy's diplomatic mail pouch?

Only if the items sent are work-related. Even so, you must ask your Associate Peace Corps Director (APCD) or Country Director (CD) for approval. The diplomatic pouch is the embassy's tool for sending packages and letters—protected by diplomatic immunity from search or seizure—back and forth from the States. Pouches come and go with varying frequency, depending on the country, ranging anywhere from daily to weekly. The diplomatic pouch is exponentially safer than the local mail system for all the reasons I describe in question 39.

Peace Corps volunteers are not granted access to the diplomatic pouch as a rule. However, if you need information for your project, tools available only in the States, documents or grant applications for planned work programs, and so on, you can request permission from your APCD or CD to use the pouch. In one instance, for example, a Peace Corps volunteer's work boots had worn out to the point where they were basically useless. He needed boots to visit farms and trek long distances to accomplish his work objectives, so he was granted permission to have a pair sent from REI in Seattle to the embassy via the diplomatic pouch. They arrived within weeks, which to those of us who had been sending and receiving packages all the while through the local postal system, seemed nothing short of miraculous.

41

Can I get magazine subscriptions sent to me?

As I mentioned in question 39, the mail system in many Peace Corps countries is anything but reliable. You can have subscriptions forwarded to your overseas address but don't count on receiving every issue. The ones that do arrive may be months old by the time you get them. What you'll need to do is call the magazine before you leave the States and give them the address of the Peace Corps office in the capital city. They may or may not require you to pay extra for postage. In some cases, they will forward the remainder of your subscription to the overseas address until it runs out without additional charges, but when you try to renew by mail they will ask for an extra twenty or thirty dollars to cover international shipping costs.

One of Peace Corps' surprise perks is a free subscription to *Newsweek* magazine—a tradition that dates back to 1982. They come in bulk to the Peace Corps offices and are distributed to volunteers' local mailboxes from there. That said, as of this writing, the Peace Corps has begun notifying volunteers that this perk may be discontinued, partly due to budgetary constraints and partly in recognition of the increasing prevalence of the Internet and online access to news and information worldwide.

Besides subscriptions, you can ask anyone sending you a care package to include a favorite magazine or two. You'd be surprised how entertaining and informative magazines can be when you have so much time to read and digest them. Internet access or not, magazines are one of those few tactile media sources that you can flip through at your leisure and share with friends and colleagues in your community. They are also a great way to stay in touch with U.S. culture, politics, music, and sports during your time away.

42

Will I be able to call the States?

This question is mostly for PCVs that end up being posted to sites without cell phone networks or reception. Otherwise, please refer to question 45 on cell phone use and access overseas.

The short answer is "yes," you will be able to call home, even if you don't have a cell phone. The difficulty will be finding the nearest phone, figuring out the billing system, and making the extremely long-distance connection over often antiquated and inadequate lines. Some volunteers end up in countries where landline phones are in every town and village. Some may even have telephones in their houses. For the most part, though, expect to be posted in a rural village with the nearest working landline connection a few hours away by bus or taxi.

Once you locate a phone, you'll probably have a few options for making the call home (or anywhere, for that matter). In many countries, there are both public telephone booths and "teleboutiques." The former often require phone cards, which come in varying denominations ranging anywhere from the equivalent of one to ten dollars. They work much like the prepaid phone cards you can purchase here in the States. Their value is encoded on a magnetic strip on the back of the card, and once you insert it into the pay phone and connect with whomever you are calling, a digital meter will start counting down until the value reaches zero, at which point you are disconnected. You can buy phone cards at post offices and local stores—though if you buy them from private vendors, be wary of counterfeits or cards that have already been used.

Teleboutiques are often the preferred way to call home, especially if you frequent the same one and get to know the owner. They are small, privately run businesses that specialize in charging people to make and receive calls and faxes. Often there will be a private booth or two, with a phone connected to a meter. You make the call, then pay the owner for the units used, as indicated by the meter. Be sure to ask and agree on the per-unit charge before you make the call or, like with so many transactions between Peace Corps volunteers and local businesses, you'll lose your shirt.

In either case, teleboutique or pay phone, you may or may not be able to use an AT&T or Sprint-type calling card. It just depends on the service area of your provider. Before you head overseas, check with your calling card company to see if they have an access code for the country you'll be traveling to. If they do, it will be much less expensive than dialing direct and you'll be able to make the call with the assistance of an English-speaking operator. If they don't, don't worry, there are still tricks to help you call home cheaply.

Regardless of whether you call from a pay phone or a teleboutique, the best way to save money is to arrange for a callback. Since calling the States from a foreign country is often three or four times more expensive than calling that same country from the States, it makes sense to have someone at home call you. Most volunteers will go to a pay phone or teleboutique, dial home, connect with a voice on the other end, and speak as fast as they can to relay the fact that (a) they are alive and healthy, (b) they are at a working phone and will be there for the next few minutes, and (c) the person they want to speak with should call them back immediately. Then they slam the phone down and find out how much those three precious minutes cost them. In Cameroon, it was between six and ten dollars, depending on where I called from and the exact amount of time I took.

Then you sit, wait, and hope that whoever is trying to call you back has luck with the international phone lines. The lines are often busy, and receiving the callback may take ten to fifteen minutes, or it may not come at all. In the meantime, you have to rabidly fend off other customers who need to use the phone, lest they tie up the line on your end.

When you do receive the callback, you will not be charged if you are at a pay phone (just as you would not be charged to receive a call at a pay phone in the States). If you are at a teleboutique, you may have to pay a small fee for tying up the line, but I encourage you to try to strike a deal with the owner. Tell him or her that if you are allowed to receive calls from the States free of charge, you will always make your long-distance calls there, and you will recommend the tele-boutique to all of your Peace Corps friends in the region.

As I mentioned in question 39, several Peace Corps programs have established regional rest houses in provincial capitals or towns that are accessible to clusters of volunteers. These houses usually provide lodging for folks that come to town to shop, bank, hang out, call home, recover from illness, or whatever. Many of these houses also have phones that can't dial out but can receive calls. Volunteers with access to such phones often call home from a nearby pay phone, but arrange to have the other party call them at the rest house, where they can hold conversations in a more relaxed and private environment. Calling home in the Peace Corps is a real treat; you'll want to do all you can to make it easy to connect and communicate.

Part VIII

Peace Corps Gadgets and Technology

43

Will I have access to the Internet?

As we rely increasingly on the Internet to conduct various aspects of our daily lives, the proposition of spending two years completely "disconnected" can be daunting. How can one manage without online shopping, blogging, surfing, skyping, emailing, downloading, browsing, file sharing, searching, chatting, and so on? With each passing year, our dependence on the Net as a medium for communicating with the broader world spreads wider and deeper. At the same time, we expect access to become easier, cheaper, and faster—and for the most part, that accurately defines the trend in the developed world.

Although information technology is undoubtedly much more prevalent across the globe than it was even five years ago, the same cannot be said of the developing world. There are still plenty of Peace Corps posts where accessing a basic telephone—much less a computer—requires substantial travel, cost, and effort. That said, the availability of Internet access in the field will depend on which region of the world, which country, and which post you are assigned to.

According to global statistics compiled by the Peace Corps, a vast majority of volunteers (74 percent) never have access to email or the Internet from their houses. More than half (60 percent) also lack access from their work sites. Of course, regional breakdowns paint a different picture. By way of generalization, many Eastern European countries are hooked into the Internet now, even at local levels. Volunteers sent to Eastern Europe are also more likely to be placed in or near bigger towns and cities, increasing the chances that they will have access to the Net. The same is true in parts of the Mediterranean and Asia. In other regions of the developing world (particularly Africa, Latin America, and the Pacific), you may need to travel to the nearest big town to find an Internet café—and once you find it, connectivity may be slow and expensive, hardware and software may be several generations old, and reliability may be sketchy, at best.

Regardless of where you serve, Internet access will be available to you at the Peace Corps office in the capital city. The Peace Corps has a policy of providing at least one fully connected desktop for every twenty-five volunteers in the field and has already rolled out this initiative worldwide. The concept is to provide a ready resource for PCVs to use for soliciting and sharing technical information on programs, connecting with colleagues on project-based requirements, communicating with home, and so on. You can expect to find a bank of computers in a "lounge" that will include Internet access, printers, scanners, and maybe even VOIP, as well as Adobe Photoshop, Pagemaker, Illustrator, and the MS suite.

Of course, you may only come into the office once or twice every quarter, so these computers won't be a regular means of communication or information exchange. Peace Corps is trying now to place computers in remote offices, closer to the volunteers who need them, and has already done so in several countries (Namibia, Micronesia, Paraguay, Bolivia, the Dominican Republic, El Salvador, Fiji, and Senegal, to name a few). If this program expands worldwide, it would be an important step toward greater uniformity among PC posts for Internet access.

44

Should I bring my laptop?

More and more PCVs are toting along portable computers as tools for work, play, and time management—and for good reasons. In the field, a laptop can be indispensable for grant and report writing, keeping a journal, composing letters, managing project budgets or spreadsheets, playing games, storing music and photos, watching movies, and so on. If you are contemplating bringing your laptop, and you use it a lot here in the States, I'd say go for it. But understand a few things first. The biggest problem will be Internet connectivity. As I mentioned earlier, Web access at the village level is still a rarity in the majority of PC countries, so don't bank on maintaining a blog or keeping up with world events online from your front porch unless you happen to be assigned to a location with reliable (and affordable) connectivity.

Depending on where you go, you may also end up subjecting your computer to extreme weather conditions (heat, rain, dust, humidity, and so on). You will be transporting your equipment over great distances under less than ideal travel conditions (bush taxis, crowded buses, overnight trains). Once you get to your final destination, there may or may not be electricity, and there will almost certainly not be a repair shop in the event that your computer breaks down. Plus, odds are low that there will be accessories available locally (or at affordable prices) for things like printers, scanners, webcams, replacement batteries, external speakers, and so on, so you'll either need to pack your own or do without.

Another potential problem at the local level is theft. As I mentioned in question 20, your house will already be a target for break-ins by virtue of the fact that you, an American, live there. When word spreads that you have a computer and accessories worth thousands of dollars in your humble abode, that target will become bigger, requiring you to take additional security precautions.

There were times when I wished I had brought a laptop with me just to streamline some of my work, especially grant writing for secondary projects. It's definitely not a necessity, but it could prove worthwhile assuming nothing goes wrong. As I mention in question 46, a laptop would also help you make the most of your other gadgets (MP3 players, digital cameras, GPS units, and so on) by allowing for content management and providing a backup for data. If you have your doubts about bringing yours, you may want to leave it behind until you've scoped out your post and its amenities. Then you can have it hand delivered by a visiting guest or a volunteer returning from home leave.

45

Will I be able to use a cell phone in the field?

One of the most incredible transformations across the face of the developing world has been the spread of cell phone use and network availability as this "leapfrog" technology has proven to be both cheap and efficient. It is not uncommon nowadays to see rural women in vegetable markets plying their trade as they chat on cell phones or send text messages from their stalls. Booths offering talk time or cell phone charging services line the sides of streets next to vendors selling plastic buckets or fresh-picked mangos. In fact, when I had the opportunity to return to my Peace Corps village in Cameroon eight years after I had COS'd, the only discernable difference that I noticed was that everyone had cell phones.

Most PCVs these days (over 70 percent) have and use cell phones on a fairly regular basis. In some countries, the Peace Corps will issue phones to its volunteers, along with calling plans on local networks that include generous talk time and text messaging (SMS) capabilities. If your phone is lost or stolen (a fairly common occurrence), it will be replaced free of charge. Cell phones even come with voice-mail service, which is nice when you miss calls from home or from the Peace Corps administration. Although the phones are meant to enable and facilitate work in the field, the Peace Corps also understands that they are tools for staying connected with friends and family, which is encouraged to the extent that it is not detrimental to your volunteer experience. Cell phones are also indispensable resources for safety and security, providing reliable communication lines between volunteers in the field and the Peace Corps office in the capital, and as a means for PCVs to call for help or emergency medical services, if needed.

As I mentioned earlier, cell phones are usually SMS-enabled, which is a boon since sending and receiving text messages costs a fraction of a voice call. In fact, most volunteers report that text messaging is the most common way they kept in touch with fellow PCVs in the field. Cell phones can also be used for international calls, though often the associated charges are very expensive (and not included in local plans). To do this, PCVs buy calling cards with prepaid minutes, which can be used for making quick calls to the States (long enough to ask whomever you are calling to call you back, since receiving calls is often much cheaper than initiating them—see question 42).

If you discover, once you know your country of assignment, that the Peace Corps does not issue phones to its volunteers there, you may choose to bring your own. Do some research on national coverage data, paying particular attention to the availability of networks in rural areas, and talk to RPCVs who have served there recently to see how prevalent cell phones are (or are becoming). Although almost three-quarters of PCVs have cell phones, 85 percent of them experience problems with poor reception in-country. Also make sure you buy a tri-band or quadra-band GSM phone (that is, one that accepts SIM cards), and make sure it is unlocked. Multi-band phones will ensure operability virtually anywhere in the world, and unlocked models will allow you to insert a SIM card from a local service provider without any problems.

46

Should I bring a digital camera? GPS unit? MP3 player?

Many PCVs these days are packing a host of digital gadgets into their bags to help make their volunteer experiences more fun, interactive, and high-tech. Although arguably not "necessities," they also provide ways to record your overseas experiences, share them with friends and family back home, and stay at least a bit plugged-in during two years in which you'll mostly be in a tech vacuum. Some of the gadgets may also have dual use, providing entertainment at home but serving as resources or valuable tools in the field.

Digital cameras are fast becoming the norm for volunteers seeking to record their experiences and share them either in print or online with folks back in the States. Although they offer a level of versatility unmatched by their film-fed counterparts (such as video recording), they also come with challenges for PCVs, including file storage and software compatibility. To deal with the file storage issue, many volunteers periodically burn CDs on their laptops, in the Peace Corps office, or at friends' houses, or they tote extra memory cards to hold them over until they can download and erase. Others pack external hard drives for transferring files, which can later be uploaded, shared, or burned. If the Peace Corps office is your primary access point to computers, bear in mind that there are often strict regulations governing software use on those PCs, so you may not be able to transfer files without some creative work-around.

MP3 players (including iPods) are increasingly popular as well. As with digital cameras, you'll need to either bring a laptop, external hard drive, or have access to a reliable PC in order to refresh your music, manage playlists, add songs, or download new content. Otherwise I'd recommend bringing a player with the most memory you can find, so as not to tire of your music (and video) selections over the course of your two years overseas.

More outdoorsy, adventurous, or safety conscious PCVs are now packing along handheld GPS units as part of their gear. As anyone who has one in their car knows, they are invaluable tools for making sure you never get lost, no matter where you are or where you are going. Unlike cell phones, GPS units don't require access to national grids or networks and require no monthly service plans, so as long as you have fairly unobstructed access to the sky and the constellation of orbiting satellites that can track you, you should be able to use them without difficulty.

Common Peace Corps issues with all electronic gadgetry include durability and battery life. As with laptops, bear in mind the heavy toll that heat, dust, humidity, and rough travel can take on high-tech equipment, and try to bring either rugged models or tough carrying cases. Also consider low-tech alternatives which, though seemingly obsolete in the States, are still in widespread use in the developing world (film cameras and CD players are everywhere in many PC countries, offering advantages in terms of compatibility, repair, and replacement options). With regard to battery life, many of the latest gadgets are dual voltage with rechargeable batteries. This is great, assuming you have electricity, but remember to bring at least a few plug adaptors so you can connect them to local outlets. If you don't have electricity at your post, you'll need to either find the nearest outlet and plan accordingly—perhaps charging when you visit the closest big town—or invest in alternatives like solar chargers, hand-cranked chargers, or battery-fed chargers.

47

Do I need a shortwave radio?

Speaking of low-tech alternatives, no matter where you are going you should bring a shortwave radio. They are easily transportable, energy efficient (some take only two to four AA batteries, which last for months under constant use), and a source of both entertainment and information when you are at your post. You'll be able to pick up local stations to tune into the culture and language, and you'll be able to pick up VOA (Voice of America) and BBC (British Broadcasting Corporation) to stay abreast of international news, including news from home.

Though I was never a big radio listener in the States, I listened to my shortwave every day in the Peace Corps. I became familiar with the programming of stations like VOA and BBC, and found myself tuning into certain broadcasts with all the enthusiasm and dedication of an NFL fan on a Monday night in the States. Many volunteers even conceded that listening to their shortwave radios overseas helped keep them better informed of world politics and current affairs than they had been at home.

Shortwave radios are expensive—they run about one hundred dollars for a good one—but as with other gadgets and electronics, the ones you buy here will be far more reliable than ones you may find overseas at comparable prices. And when you leave the Peace Corps, you can often sell your shortwave radio to an incoming volunteer or give it as a treasured gift to a friend in the village. My only advice is to shop around and don't let the cost scare you away. For the weight, it may turn out to be the best and most valuable item you bring.

Part IX

The Social Scene

48

How close will I live to another volunteer?

In many Peace Corps countries, several volunteers are assigned to the same village. In others, you may be a short trip away from your nearest neighbor. It's rare to be so isolated that you won't at least have the option of visiting a fellow volunteer if you want or need to. Overall, the Peace Corps tries to cluster volunteers close together in an effort to create a support network that benefits the volunteer and the program by fostering happier, more productive workers. As reported in the 2006 Peace Corps Volunteer Survey Report, 71 percent of PCVs live within thirty kilometers of another volunteer, while 82 percent can reach the nearest PCV in less than two hours. Twenty-three percent are only five kilometers or less from their nearest Peace Corps neighbor, while 29 percent are over thirty kilometers away (Peace Corps Office of Planning, Policy and Analysis, March 23, 2007).

In cases where the Peace Corps places more than one volunteer in a village or town, often the volunteers aren't in the same program. One may be doing forestry, one could be a health volunteer, and another could be doing community development. With folks who are clustered with other volunteers, it's a crapshoot as to whether everyone will get along or end up avoiding each other. Individual personalities play a big role in determining interactions. One thing to keep in mind if you are assigned a post-mate or two, however, is that there is a danger in relying too heavily on other volunteers for company and support, thereby delaying or inhibiting the process of acculturation and adjustment. The temptation of having someone right there with whom you can speak English, talk about familiar things, listen to familiar music, and create a detached environment from your foreign and intimidating surroundings may be powerful. But for those who do strike a balance and successfully cultivate village friendships, colleagues, and interests, it can be a tremendous comfort to have a friend and fellow volunteer with whom to share so many experiences.

When the Peace Corps puts just one volunteer in each village, PCVs will likely find that they are within a couple hours' journey of the nearest volunteer, as mentioned earlier. That journey may be by bike, bus, train, foot, or car, and may take much longer depending on weather, breakdowns, delays, and other unforeseen factors, but it will be comforting to know that you can reach someone familiar (culturally speaking) within a relatively short period of time if the need arises. And it probably will. In my case, the closest volunteer was about two hours north of me. We got together at least twice a month to cook spaghetti dinners, listen to music, play cribbage, go for hikes, talk about our experiences and anxieties, attend social functions in the village, share work experiences, and plan vacations and trips. There were times when I visited that person because I wanted to, and times when I did so because I needed to. Make use of your fellow volunteers when you're overseas; they will help make the experience both easier and more memorable.

49

How often will I see
other volunteers?

It goes without saying that if you have post-mates, you will have substantially greater opportunities to see other volunteers than if you don't. That said, the amount of interaction you have with other volunteers once you are assigned to your village is really up to you. There will undoubtedly be times when you feel the need to see a fellow volunteer. Perhaps you'll be looking for someone to whom you can vent in "American English" when you encounter frustrations at post; or you may want to share a great cultural experience with someone who understands the magnitude and importance of that event without explanation. When you're feeling down or homesick, you may want the company of someone who can commiserate with you. Or you may want someone you can invite to share in a village ceremony, someone with whom you can relive that moment later in life. There will also be times when you get sick and want someone to lean on who has been there and knows what it's like. In essence, there will be times when you'll most likely feel compelled to seek out familiar ground and the comforting presence of a fellow volunteer.

Aside from those times, however, it really varies based on personalities and preferences. Whether you intend to stay put in your village or town and avoid Peace Corps parties, trips, and functions, or you decide to participate fully in every Peace Corps event throughout the two years, is your call. There will be parties at people's posts and in centralized locations where people can meet up easily. There will be vacations and trips (officially sanctioned and clandestine) to take. There will be numerous opportunities to participate in official committees, training courses, ceremonies, and administrative volunteer groups that revolve around the Peace Corps office in the capital. I knew volunteers who avoided all of that and left their villages only when absolutely necessary, and others who divided their time among their village, their Peace Corps friends, and their commitments to Peace Corps' extra-curricular committees and planning groups.

Your experience will be what you make of it, and your interactions with other volunteers in relation to the time spent in your village can make a difference. As with most other aspects of Peace Corps life where you will face choices and decisions that have an impact, my advice is to try to strike a balance. I found it important to maintain ties and friendships with my Peace Corps colleagues, and many of those friendships are proving to be lifelong. I also fostered meaningful and enriching friendships in my village, without which I wouldn't have been able to work and live so far from home for two years. Though you may feel pressure from the Peace Corps administration to stay at your post and minimize your interactions with other volunteers, and you may feel pressure from your Peace Corps friends to maximize interactions with them at the expense of your life in the village, have in mind the way you want your experience to be and strive to attain it.

50

What is the drug and alcohol situation like?

Many who join the Peace Corps are shocked to discover how prevalent drug and alcohol use is within the volunteer community. Pressure to drink or smoke often bombards volunteers from several angles. Drugs and alcohol may be cheap, abundant, and freely consumed by fellow volunteers during social events. Within a volunteer's host community, local customs and traditions may revolve around shared drinking experiences (for example, imbibing freshly tapped palm wine, recently fermented corn beer, homemade vodka, and so on). Inevitable periods of boredom or depression at post may prompt volunteers to use alcohol or drugs as a means of escape.

The Peace Corps addresses this topic only briefly during training. They admonish volunteers against succumbing to pressure from peers, counterparts, or their village environments. They also give you the official line on Peace Corps policy, which is that even suspected drug use may be cause for separation, and excessive drinking may result in administrative reprimands, warnings, or termination of service.

The fact is, in some countries and Peace Corps programs, to drink in your village or do drugs with other volunteers presents itself as a quick and effective way to acculturate or gain acceptance at a time in your life when "fitting in" has never before meant so much. As a way of dealing with boredom or loneliness at post, drugs and alcohol are attractive alternatives for many. If you aren't aware of the dangers associated with approaching cultural and social immersion from that angle, or if you fail to see the pitfalls in avoiding or creatively coping with moments of boredom and inactivity in your village, it can be a disaster. Aside from the negative health and psychological effects associated with drug and alcohol use, volunteers under the influence may compromise their safety and security by engaging in high-risk activities, such as practicing unsafe sex or instigating fights.

What can you do? Be aware that, especially during your first few months in training and at post, you will be psychologically vulnerable and eager to adapt to your new environment. Be aware that drinking or doing drugs may seem to be a real door opener for gaining acceptance from your peers and from the people in your village. Be aware that some volunteers go overboard and come to rely on alcohol or drugs to get them through their whole two years. Be aware of any severe changes in your drinking or drug use patterns, and use the Peace Corps medical office for counseling or assistance if you suspect you have (or are developing) a problem.

Make a list of things to do at post when you are bored or have time to kill (cooking, tuning your bike, reading, writing letters, learning to play the harmonica, updating your journal, taking pictures, hiking and exploring, visiting friends, and so on). And don't forget who you are; it's good to bend once in a while to experience something new, but be careful not to break.

51
What is the dating scene like in the Peace Corps?

It is alive and kicking. Peace Corps volunteers date other Peace Corps volunteers all the time. And the reasons are fairly obvious. You have a small number of people with certain common interests and goals, living far from home and sharing intense life experiences for two years. In that kind of environment, it doesn't take long for friendships to blossom into intimate relationships. Some of those intimate relationships last only a night; others end up lasting a lifetime.

Although at first you may look around at your fellow trainees and marvel at how different everyone seems from you, soon after arriving in-country you'll transcend those differences and see that there is, indeed, a common thread that connects most volunteers. As you begin to rely on your friendships with others to help make training more manageable and meaningful, you also begin to see how easy it is for closer relationships to form.

In addition to environmental and personality factors, there is also the hormonal factor. Most Peace Corps volunteers are young adults who find that self-imposed abstinence is hardly a palliative for the social and cultural isolation imposed upon them by their foreign surroundings. Intervolunteer hookups don't always end after training either. Peace Corps parties, extended visits from other volunteers, and other gatherings (formal and informal) over the two years offer numerous opportunities to strike up a romance or two.

For as long as the Peace Corps has existed, volunteers have also had intimate relationships with host country nationals. Just as sure as someone in your training group will eventually date another volunteer, someone else will date an HCN before the two years are up. Officially the Peace Corps doesn't say much on this topic. They focus instead on encouraging safe sex, regardless of who your partner is (for more on this topic, see question 35).

Aside from the health aspect, keep in mind your professional obligations to the Peace Corps and make sure personal relationships don't compromise them. If you're attracted to the chief's daughter, for example, but you know that a failed relationship with her would put you on the village's "most wanted" list, think twice before striking up a romance. A volunteer in my group alienated himself from his local community by dating a woman who flaunted their relationship to her peers. Other villagers became jealous of her and spiteful toward him, to the point where it substantially impeded his efforts to accomplish project-related goals. Peace Corps ended up transferring him to another village in a different part of the country (his girlfriend went with him). It seemed to be an administrative headache, though they were both happy in the end.

One aspect of Peace Corps dating that you may find grossly unappealing is the associated gossip network. As with a small college or company here in the States, word travels quickly among friends and colleagues. You may think you've begun a clandestine relationship with your neighbor or the volunteer three villages away, but rest assured the Peace Corps grapevine will transmit that information to the far reaches of the country before you can bat an eye. Cell phone reception may not exist, the mail system may be primeval, and volunteers may be separated by vast distances—but gossip in the Peace Corps seems to have its own high-speed bandwidth. Of course, as with any grapevine, the information about volunteers that races around the country is rarely accurate or reliable. But to a group of people hungry for news and entertainment, it serves a purpose and knows no mercy, so consider yourself forewarned.

52

What happens if I want to marry a host country national?

When you spend two years in a small community getting to know local customs, languages, traditions, and people, opportunities arise to meet special people and form close relationships that may grow into lifelong commitments. The Peace Corps does not officially support or discourage such relationships; they only insist that you meet your obligations to the organization and keep personal issues from compromising your programmatic responsibilities. The Peace Corps' primary requirement concerning volunteer marriages to HCNs is that the CD be informed so that a determination can be made regarding potential conflicts with continued service. As part of that determination, your spouse would need to pass a security investigation (national agency check) and demonstrate that any employment they hold is not in conflict with the goals and mission of the Peace Corps.

I attended a number of weddings between PCVs and HCNs while I was in-country. They were joyous occasions, attended by relatives of the bride and groom, fellow volunteers, Peace Corps staff, and local friends. In most cases, the newlyweds flew to the States after the PCV finished service to begin a new life together. Though there are no statistics on success or divorce rates resulting from Peace Corps marriages to HCNs, the couples I knew seemed well matched and happy, impressing me with the unpredictable and powerful ways the Peace Corps may impact one's life.

Part X

The Toughest Job You'll Ever Love?

53
What is the work schedule like?

It depends on your program. Education volunteers are tied to their school's schedules, working during school terms and vacationing during holidays and term breaks. Health volunteers working at clinics may be expected to put in full days. Agriculture and forestry volunteers tailor their work schedules to accommodate the seasons, the farmers' schedules, crop rotations, and so on.

In my case, I tended to spend around two or three hours per day, four days per week with individual farmers practicing hands-on agroforestry. I spent another few hours each week providing demonstrations or "extensions" (training seminars) to groups of farmers. The rest of my time was divided among secondary projects, socializing (which is, as your trainers will tell you, part of your job), and doing my own thing.

In truth, you will have a great deal of independence and flexibility when setting your schedule, so a lot will rest on your initiative and willingness to work. As long as you are accomplishing your project goals and being productive at post, the Peace Corps administration won't breathe down your neck. Just take care not to abuse the independence—there have been cases in which wayward volunteers were sent packing due to insufficient work-related progress at post.

During training, you'll be told that Peace Corps is a twenty-four-hour-a-day, seven-day-a-week job. To a degree, that is true. When you are at your post, the line between work and leisure can often be thin. Socializing with farmers or fellow teachers is as important to developing effective working relationships as meeting them on the farm or at school. Attending community celebrations or local ceremonies may do more for promoting your projects than months of fieldwork and demonstrations. In the Peace Corps, your identity is so closely tied to your organization and its objectives that it's hard not to see links between your social activities and your "official" responsibilities.

54

How much supervision is there for volunteers in the field?

Not a lot. Once you get to your village, you have a degree of independence that few other jobs offer. You can be as proactive or inactive as you want. You have the opportunity and authority to design, implement, manage, and monitor entire programs with little, if any, intervention from the Peace Corps office. They are there to guide you, and serve as a technical resource if you need them, but they will not manage your work while you are in the field.

Your APCD will try to visit your post at least once every six months. That's four times during your entire two years. As such, your day-to-day schedule and your overall work-related accomplishments will depend on your initiative and level of motivation (see question 53). There may be a Peace Corps volunteer leader (PCVL) nearby to help you with technical difficulties you encounter, but even that person will not be "supervising" you in the traditional sense of the word. In the event that you slack to an unacceptable degree and your programs suffer as a result, your APCD can put you on a Performance Improvement Plan (PIP). PIPs provide written performance targets and document your improvement (or lack thereof), and aim to either resolve the problem or justify administrative separation.

My advice is to take advantage of Peace Corps' unique work environment to gain invaluable project experience and develop useful self-management skills. Remind yourself that, in your next job, you may be squeezed into a rigid corporate or bureaucratic hierarchy, constantly reacting to edicts from above and competing to get ahead. In the Peace Corps, there is no ladder. Volunteers work independently at post and are empowered to start secondary projects, apply for grants, conduct public outreach and education campaigns, evaluate project successes, and much more.

At the same time, take advantage of the independence to meet personal goals. Travel, visit friends, see the country, relax, and enjoy life as only a freewheelin' PCV can. Too many Peace Corps volunteers get so locked into their work and projects at post that their two years pass them by before they realize how little of the country they've seen and how much of the culture remains unexplored.

Be social, participate in Peace Corps committees and training opportunities, throw parties for your neighbors, have visitors, and take vacations. Find a comfortable balance point between work and play, and stay there.

55

Will I work with other international development agencies while I'm overseas?

You may. There are numerous development agencies operating overseas and, depending on where you serve, you may encounter one or several of them at your post. They may be working on projects that overlap with your program; they may be focusing on entirely separate issues. They may maintain a staff of twenty people, complete with Land Rovers and computers; they may consist of one guy and his notepad. They may welcome you and invite you to collaborate; they may have a disdain for Peace Corps volunteers or feel protective of their projects.

The Peace Corps does not discourage volunteers from collaborating with other development agencies, provided that the work is relevant to the volunteers' primary or secondary projects and doesn't usurp all of their time. If you find a nongovernmental organization (NGO) to collaborate with, take care to avoid becoming "free labor" by overextending yourself and avoid the appearance of working for it rather than for the Peace Corps.

You should also be aware of the NGO's reputation in your work area before you agree to collaborate. It may be that its approach toward development is more top-down and resource-intensive than grassroots and labor-intensive. If so, people in your town or village may perceive the organization as an elitist outsider that imposes development rather than encourages it.

If you do manage to find a group that seems worthy of collaboration, and the group is amenable to the idea, consider it a good opportunity to enrich your Peace Corps experience. Working together will assuredly multiply the impact of your efforts, while exposing you to professional contacts and experiences that could prove valuable even after your service with the Peace Corps is over. You'll undoubtedly learn more about development, learn more about NGO administration, and discover new techniques to accomplish project goals. Similarly it boosts the Peace Corps' exposure to sister agencies and encourages cooperation between PCVs and NGOs in the future.

56

Is the Peace Corps effective as a development agency?

Here's a whole can of worms that, if opened, could fill the pages of a book by itself. Does the Peace Corps work? Does it accomplish its aims? Does it effect positive change at the grassroots level? In some respects, yes; in others, not really. When I was there, serving my two years overseas, I thought it almost ludicrous to imagine that my efforts mattered to anyone but me. I had little faith in my work as effecting lasting, positive change on my village, much less the country of Cameroon. I felt my own ambitions and goals were being fulfilled for the most part, while the greater goals of "development" and "intercultural exchange" consisted mostly of administrative rhetoric.

Of course, those were impressions from the field, amid daily struggles with the basics of life in a developing country. It's hard to think objectively about the big picture when you're living in a small, relatively isolated corner of the world. Now that I'm back and have had time to reflect on the entire experience, I see my life in Cameroon as having impacted the people with whom I lived and worked in a much broader and more definable way.

It's true—no volunteer is going to leave his or her post having single-handedly saved a rain forest or boosted a nation's economy. No volunteer will COS having reversed national trends in infant mortality. No volunteer will be able to claim they succeeded in dispelling all the myths and stereotypes about Americans in their host communities. But each volunteer should be able to look back at their Peace Corps experience and put their finger on a few lives they helped better and minds they helped broaden. When they do that, they will realize the enormity of their accomplishments and the impressive effect those changes have on a larger scale.

Peace Corps volunteers have a tough mission to begin with; they are charged with the onerous duty of improving lives at the grassroots level in parts of the world where change may not only be impractical but also impossible. They must promote intercultural exchange and introduce new ways of tackling important social and environmental issues, often in societies dubious of the message, methods, and even motive. They are deprived of the material and monetary means that other development agencies rely upon to facilitate that change, and are left only with technical knowledge and an elemental ability to inspire change through collaboration and education. Given such formidable hurdles in accomplishing the agency's goals, it's no wonder so many PCVs question their contribution to "development" in the academic sense of the word. For most, development emerges as a tangent to the everyday relationships and experiences of village life.

Ideally Peace Corps volunteers integrate so well into their communities that they are able to work creatively from the inside out. They make friends with their colleagues, they make use of available resources, they rely on cultural exchange and dialogue to bridge technical and resource gaps. Such an approach inevitably produces a more sustainable and widespread change—though from the field, volunteers rarely have the vantage point to appreciate it. Although the agency's goals are not always met by each volunteer and program, a testament to the organization's overall impact is the demand for volunteers by host country governments and the widespread (bipartisan) approval of the Peace Corps here in the United States.

57

What are some common criticisms of the Peace Corps?

While, on the whole, the Peace Corps is viewed as an important federal institution worthy of its budget and directive, there are those who argue for funding cutbacks and organizational changes. Similarly, although most would characterize PCVs as exemplary citizens making tremendous sacrifices for noble causes, others question volunteers' motives and doubt their contributions.

The harshest criticisms of the Peace Corps often come from PCVs or RPCVs themselves, stemming from their direct exposure to critical aspects of the organization and its services. Their comments run the gamut—from arguing that the Peace Corps experience is too long to arguing that it isn't long enough; from petitioning for greater funding for grassroots projects to lamenting the elevated status of volunteers in the village whose monthly stipends are deemed excessive. Many volunteers feel that the Peace Corps' training program should provide more technical guidance. Others call for less administrative and programmatic direction for volunteers in the field. Some are convinced that the Peace Corps' prime directive (and hidden agenda) is to serve U.S. foreign policy interests, to the detriment of its development efforts. Still others point to limitations that volunteer attrition and turnover have on sustainability, and claim that Peace Corps projects are not participatory enough. All of the above criticisms have merit and ring true to an extent. If you flip forward to question 74 though, you may get a sense of how quickly those sentiments soften with time.

Critics outside of the Peace Corps' family circle largely target volunteers' motives and the agency's capability to effect lasting change. The stereotype of PCVs as hippie throwbacks with too much free time on their hands is sometimes embraced by these detractors. They not only pigeonhole the volunteer experience as yet another thrill for college grads, but also wonder what contributions to third world development a twenty-two-year-old fine arts major can truly make. They point to the failures of relatively affluent development agencies such as the World Bank, the U.S. Agency for International Development (USAID), or the United Nations Development Program (UNDP) and wonder how, in comparison, a nickel-and-dime operation like the Peace Corps can combat issues of global import. And finally, critics insist that Peace Corps volunteers themselves are the prime beneficiaries of their service abroad. For PCVs, they argue, the experience is an opportunity to learn another language, see some of the world, and enrich their personal worldview, all on the taxpayers' bill. For HCNs, they say, it provides a succession of random Americans intruding on their culture, living off of their generosity, and leaving once the novelty wears off.

As you consider joining, factor in the criticisms of the Peace Corps, but keep in mind that the organization is generally praised for its persistence in educating and helping the world, one person at a time. As I mention in question 71, no matter what you learn about the Peace Corps during your two years—its ups and downs, its bright spots and blemishes—you'll quickly realize that most people in the States have a much simpler, nobler impression of the organization. No development agency is flawless, but the Peace Corps' reputation and longevity attest to its overall success.

Part XI

Rules to Live By— Peace Corps Policy

58

Will I be able to have friends and family visit from the States?

Yes, and I highly recommend you do so. You will possess a thorough knowledge of the language, culture, and geography of your country of service, and will therefore be able to show them around like few others can. As expensive as the round-trip ticket may be, once they get there they will pay virtually nothing for food or lodging. You will have a network of Peace Corps friends scattered throughout the country with whom you and your guests will be able to stay. You'll be "up" on which food is good, which is bad, which is cheap, and which is a real treat. You'll be able to bargain for them in the local language to secure deals on souvenirs and gifts. You'll know how to travel like locals—on bush taxis, trains, buses—which, in and of itself, is half the adventure and fun. And the list goes on . . .

Now the technicalities: you are not supposed to take vacation days during your first or last three months at post (see question 67). This means, unless you plan on leaving your visitors behind while you go to work every day, it isn't practical to invite people to visit then. The rest of your service is fair game. Have as many people as you want come visit (within reason), and have them stay for at least three to five weeks to make it worth their (and your) time.

Well before the trip, have your visitor get in touch with the embassy of your country in Washington, D.C., to find out how to get a visa and how much it will cost. Some countries will require a written invitation from you before issuing a tourist visa to your guests. Also, if your guests need malaria prophylaxis, have them contact their health care provider to see if it's covered through insurance.

It's often helpful to spend half an hour brainstorming a realistic packing list to send to visitors before their trip. Keep in mind the seasons, the places you plan to take them, and their baggage weight limitations. Use the opportunity to have them bring you goodies too. There's nothing like a box of Reese's Peanut Butter Cups or a package of new cotton underwear to recharge you after months of eating okra stew and watching your boxers or bras disintegrate from hundreds of hand-scrubbing washes.

You may also want to ask your visitors to reserve space in their luggage for care packages and small gifts from families of fellow volunteers. As I mention in question 39, packages sent through international and local mail systems often break or disappear. It's nice if families of volunteers can rest assured that their mail will reach its destination quickly and intact. You may want the favor returned later too.

Although it's great to have lots of visitors, and it breaks up the time nicely, keep in mind that you don't want to spend the entire two years entertaining guests and playing tour guide. Don't laugh, I know a few people who had friends and relatives from the States coming through like commuters at rush hour. When that happens, not only do you start feeling alienated from your village and work, but you also start resenting your guests and feeling that your Peace Corps experience is being compromised.

59

How often do volunteers quit before their two years are over?

The Peace Corps' global average has historically been around 10 percent. Breaking down the numbers by country, however, reveals some large variances in resignation numbers. Looking at Africa, for example, over 20 percent or more quit early in Swaziland and Chad. Jordan and Khazakstan have the highest resignation rates in the EMA region, while Belize, Guyana, Suriname, and Jamaica—yes, Jamaica—top the list for IAP. In other words, depending on where you end up, you may look around on your first day of training and expect that almost a quarter of your group will not be attending the COS conference two years down the road. (Those interested in finding stats on particular countries of assignment should visit www.peacecorpswiki.org/FOIAdocs /FY2006ETReport.pdf.)

People quit early for all kinds of reasons, none of which are invalid or trivial. Making that decision is often painful and traumatic. Although the Peace Corps doesn't encourage it, they don't discourage it either. The door to home is always left open, which can be comforting and distracting at the same time.

Leaving early in Peace Corps jargon is called "early terminating," or "ET'ing" for short. Volunteers ET for reasons as distinct and different as the individuals themselves. Some leave because they miss their boyfriends or girlfriends. Some leave because they realize they'd rather be in graduate school. Some leave because they have the misfortune of falling sick a lot and tire of worrying about their health for two years. Some leave because they discover they aren't interested in their Peace Corps program and can't fathom digging wells or weighing babies month after month. Others don't like the climate, don't like the food, don't like the music . . . who knows? Inevitably, though, you'll see a few of your fellow trainees head back home before training is over. Others will follow at various points during the two years.

People ET in waves. The first group typically leaves during training, having decided that the prospect of living and working overseas for two years is unbearable, or at least vastly different from their expectations. The second wave hits between three and six months after training—far and away the most trying and difficult period of the Peace Corps. Many refer to that period as the "make it or break it" months. After three to six months, you've either established a workload, learned more of the language, acclimated to solo living (washing clothes, hauling water, cooking food), and made friends in your community, or you haven't. If you haven't, you'll likely conclude that your lifestyle is unsustainable and you'll feel the pressure to leave.

The third and final wave hits around the one-year mark. People who ET after a year usually do so for professional or programmatic reasons. Perhaps they find their Peace Corps work unsatisfying. Perhaps their work is nonexistent and they feel they are biding their time. Perhaps they hear from graduate schools and don't want to defer admission for a year. Perhaps they feel their work sites aren't a good fit for their personalities, and they don't want to go through the ordeal of transferring and starting all over again.

Whatever the case, more people than you think ET and you can't predict who those people will be. Some of the most upbeat and optimistic trainees and volunteers may bail after a few weeks or months. Some of the most pessimistic and bitter volunteers may stay for the whole two years. It's best to withhold judgment about people that ET, especially since you may wake up one day and find that you are one of them. Just about everyone I knew seriously considered ET'ing at least once during their service. When you find yourself thinking that everything stinks—your job, your village, your life, your health, your mental attitude, your emotional state, your house, your colleagues, your program, and your country—ET'ing can look like a nice ticket to paradise. It's up to you to discourage yourself, so think hard about what you're experiencing and use your friends and family to help sort it out before jumping through a hoop that you can't go back through. If you still want to ET—go for it. No one knows what's best for you but you.

On a personal note, I should say that most (if not all) of the volunteers I knew who ET'd later came to regret it. I say this only because it struck me, when talking to these folks, how much they wished they had stuck through the two years. It wasn't until most of them reached the States that they realized life back here isn't a bed of roses either. They ended up missing friends they'd made in the Peace Corps, the diversity of culture and life in their host communities, and the exotic and sometimes surreal environments of the countries they'd left. As with everything else in life, things usually get better if you give them time. A good general rule to live by if you feel like you really want to ET is to wait a couple of weeks and see how you feel then. The option is always there—right up until the day before you officially COS. You may as well wait a while to see if things shape up or problems resolve themselves before leaving. With family emergencies and grad school acceptances, you may not have the luxury of giving yourself some time to think things over carefully. But in most other instances, I'd advise patience and processing before packing.

60

What is the procedure
for quitting early?

The Peace Corps' attitude toward volunteers who want to ET is pretty straightforward. They know that if you are unhappy, for whatever reason, you should probably go home. They may ask you once if you're sure; they may not even do that. They don't want to momentarily talk you out of leaving, only to have you to return to your post, sulk for a few more weeks, then decide to ET again. So if you come into the office to announce your decision to ET, don't do it with the hopes that your APCD will try to dissuade you.

The actual process is relatively simple. Once you announce your intent to ET, you'll go through a quick series of "exit interviews" with your APCD and CD. You'll tell them why you have decided to leave early and how you reached your decision. They'll be interested to know if your community played a factor (did your neighbors stone you every morning?), if your program played a factor (were you supposed to be teaching English in a village where the only school burned down three years ago?), or if it was something else that could be rectified by transferring you to another site or working through the problem. Keep in mind that transferring villages is no easy feat, however, and if you haven't previously approached the Peace Corps administration about moving to another post, they may not believe that "dissatisfaction with work and community" lies at the root of the problem. They'll be more likely to conclude that you simply aren't happy in the Peace Corps, and will accept your decision to ET without resistance. They will also evaluate whether your post should be replaced with another volunteer once you leave or abandoned by the Peace Corps altogether, so be careful what you say. It'll be easy to blame your village for all your woes and troubles, but think twice before pointing any fingers—you may cheat your host community out of help they need and a future volunteer out of a great experience.

Before you leave for the States, you'll need to submit to Peace Corps' COS medical examination, a thorough "systems check" designed to test for amoebas, viruses, worms, HIV, schisto, filaria, and any other diseases common to the area. The exam will take approximately two to three days. If you haven't already lugged your belongings into the office, you should get a day or two to return to your house and pack up.

When you ET, you may receive a readjustment allowance advance of $200 in-country, if authorized by the country director. You will not be given the cash-in-lieu-of-ticket option discussed in question 68. The Peace Corps will purchase your return ticket to the States and you must (barring extenuating circumstances) follow the itinerary without deviation unless you shell out your own cash to change it. In other words, you can't ET and use the return ticket to hang out in Europe for awhile or travel to Nepal. Depending on how long you served before ET'ing, and the reasons you cited for leaving early, you may still get noncompetitive eligibility for jobs in the federal government when you get back to the States (see question 72).

As the Peace Corps states in their volunteer handbook, resignations are final and may not be reconsidered or appealed. In other words, before setting the wheels in motion, make sure your decision is final and the right one for you.

61

Can I get kicked out of the Peace Corps?

There are several golden rules in the Peace Corps which, if violated, can earn you a one-way ticket home. They differ from country to country but often include the following (in no particular order):

1. Riding on a motorcycle without a helmet (or in some countries, driving or riding a motorcycle at all)

2. Failing to take any required medications (including malaria prophylaxes)

3. Crossing an international border without notifying the Peace Corps

4. Using, or being accused of using, illicit drugs

5. Entering "restricted zones"—areas the Peace Corps (and usually the U.S. embassy) have determined dangerous for one reason or another

6. Accepting money for services rendered during your Peace Corps experience

7. Involving yourself in local or national politics overseas (such as participating in rallies, protests, demonstrations, and so on)

Of course nothing is ever as simple as it seems. In order to be kicked out for the above sins, you have to be caught. I'm not trying to sound devious, but you should be aware that volunteers do violate these rules in certain circumstances and get away with it, if they use common sense.

For example, Peace Corps volunteers in countries around the world often encounter cheap and plentiful supplies of marijuana. Using discretion and subtlety, they obtain and consume it without administrative repercussions. Others cross international borders surreptitiously to visit Peace Corps friends or purchase souvenirs without declaring official vacation days. Still others opt not to take their malaria prophylaxis due to adverse physical reactions and unwanted side effects. Though all of the above, if discovered, constitute grounds for instant termination, they are practiced routinely and privately, out of sight of the Peace Corps administration.

My advice is to avoid influences or activities that may compromise your reputation or standing with Peace Corps officials. There aren't many rules in the Peace Corps, but the ones that exist are not taken lightly when broken. If you decide to bend or break a rule, do so privately and discreetly. Be sure you fully understand the risks and possible consequences of your actions, and don't expect leniency if you're caught. The Peace Corps understands and respects your rights as an adult and an individual, but when it comes to upholding regulations designed to safeguard your health and well-being, they are unyielding.

62

How many volunteers extend their service beyond the first two years?

Lots. Volunteers extend for various reasons. Some initiate projects that take longer than two years to complete—projects they feel obliged to see through to the end. Some become emotionally attached to people in their villages and find it difficult to leave for personal reasons. Some relish the relatively structure-free and independent life that the Peace Corps provides. Some decide to apply for positions as Peace Corps volunteer leaders (PCVLs) or trainers for the next group of volunteers. A few fear the upheaval and difficult process of readjusting to life in the States (see question 70).

Extending for a third year, however, is more complicated than it may seem. There are a limited number of extension slots each year, dictated by the Peace Corps' budget and annual appropriation. If you wish to extend, you must formally apply and interview with your APCD. Volunteers most likely to be approved for extensions are those whose primary reasons are work- or project-related. Those who apply for personal reasons rarely receive top priority on the extension list.

As I mentioned above, some people extend in order to become PCVLs. PCVLs are typically third-year volunteers who act as intermediaries between other volunteers in their program and their APCD. They live in a provincial capital or big town, giving them access to a cluster of volunteers. They provide personal and programmatic support by visiting volunteers in the field and helping them with technical or site-specific problems. They often live in more modern houses with electricity and phones, enabling them to contact the Peace Corps office regularly. They work closely with APCDs to coordinate meetings, conferences, and site visits, and are given a limited supervisory role over their volunteer peers.

If you decide to extend for a third year to be a PCVL, ask your APCD how and when to apply. The process can be highly competitive, as usually only the most motivated, committed, and productive volunteers express interest. You must complete a written application and interview with your APCD. Not all PCVLs love their job, so talk to your PCVL before you apply to gain some insight into the position and to help you decide if it's right for you.

If you extend, you'll be entitled to a four-week (30-day) home-leave trip between your second and third years. The Peace Corps will provide you with a round-trip ticket to the States and will pay you a modest per diem. If you don't want to visit the States, you can select another destination as long as the cost of airfare is the same or less (otherwise you must pay the difference). I knew one volunteer who spent his home leave in London, visiting his girlfriend. His family wasn't pleased, but the option was there for him to exercise.

If you ET during your third year, you are liable for the costs of the home-leave ticket and per diem. You can either repay Peace Corps directly or have the money withdrawn from your readjustment allowance. Think hard before following this route though. ET'ing in your third year vexes both the Peace Corps administration and other volunteers, because the extension process is competitive—meaning you beat someone out of a third-year spot who really wanted it.

63

Will I be overseas for the whole two years or can I come home in between?

Unless you foot the bill yourself, you are there for the whole two years. There is no R & R or home leave for PCVs, with the exception of third-year extensions (see question 62). You will have forty-eight vacation days during your volunteer service to use as you please. Several volunteers, including myself, came back to the States halfway through their two years for weddings, funerals, holidays, and the like. The costs of those trips, however, are the PCV's responsibility, and vacation days must be claimed.

Aside from extending, the only way to fly back to the States on the Peace Corps' tab is to get "medivacked" (medically evacuated). If you contract some deadly or bizarre disease, get pregnant, experience severe psychological duress, or injure yourself in such a manner that you can't be treated reasonably in-country, you may be medivacked to Washington, D.C. For more on medivacs, see question 32.

64

Can I transfer programs if I don't like what I'm doing?

Not really. When you join the Peace Corps, you state in your application the skills and relevant areas in which you have experience. When you interview, you are evaluated and considered for a specific PC program area. When you go through training, you learn technical skills and practical methods to plan, implement, and evaluate projects in your program. If, during training, you decide you aren't interested in the program and can't envision yourself doing related project work for the next two years, the Peace Corps will most likely invite you to ET. If you get to post and start your projects, then months down the road visit the office to voice similar complaints, the Peace Corps will still most likely invite you to ET. They may be able to offer you another post, but there usually isn't much they can offer in the way of other programs.

There are some extenuating circumstances that may allow you to change programs, however. For example, in my country of service there was a nationwide teachers' strike that resulted in the closing of all public schools for almost a year. This left the Peace Corps in a bind since a quarter of all volunteers in-country were education volunteers. At first, affected PCVs were advised to wait out the strike and start secondary projects in the meantime. When it became apparent that the strike was going to last more than a month or two, and volunteers were starting to ET en masse, volunteers were given some leeway in deciding if they wanted to switch programs, go to other countries, or return to the States. Those who chose to switch programs faced quite an ordeal though. In most cases they had to change villages, undergo at least a month or two of programmatic training, and start their two years all over again.

My advice is to think hard about your assigned program area before going overseas with the Peace Corps. If you have any doubts about your commitment to the program, think about reapplying under a different one. If you are intent on going despite doubts about your interest level in the work, do your best to go into it with an open mind and a positive attitude. Also, talk to RPCVs who worked in your assigned field to find out exactly what your work will entail. If you find, once you get to your post, that your area of assignment isn't exactly your cup of tea, remember that you can always throw yourself into secondary projects. They may end up being a low profile way of contributing to your community while avoiding the disfavor of Peace Corps administration.

65

Can I transfer countries if I don't like where I am?

As with transferring programs, transferring countries is only done under extenuating circumstances. In my two years as a volunteer, I only witnessed one incident that resulted in the transfer of volunteers from one country to another. A country that bordered ours erupted in civil war and all of its volunteers were evacuated to my country of service. They were housed in the capital while the Peace Corps figured out a "next step." As it happened, the evacuated volunteers were given a couple of options. Those who were interested in COS'ing were offered early COS dates, and many of them left Cameroon to go directly back to the States. Those who were relatively new volunteers or wished to continue serving overseas were given the opportunity to transfer to another country, as dictated by the availability of positions, and start their two years over again. Although country transfers aren't guaranteed, evacuees are given priority consideration for enrollment in other Peace Corps programs.

The only other real opportunity PCVs have to transfer countries comes when they extend for a third year or apply to reenroll (that is, sign up for another full two-year Peace Corps tour) as they near their COS date. With a great deal of effort, volunteers can seek out openings in other Peace Corps countries and apply for positions—often within their program area. To negotiate the transfer successfully, interested PCVs must contact appropriate CDs and maintain a similar level of persistence as was required during the initial PC application process. If you find yourself interested in attempting a transfer of this sort, start the process early in your second year to ensure enough time for the information exchange and application reviews. It's neither an easy nor common feat, but it's not altogether impossible.

66

Will I have access to embassy, commissary, and American Club services?

While you are overseas, you will quickly learn all about the "haves" and "have nots" by comparing your life with that of the embassy diplomats around you. You will be living in rudimentary structures with minimal amenities; they will be living in marble mansions with guards, servants, drivers, and gardeners. You will be eating local food and shopping in local markets; they will be eating American food and shopping in the commissary. You will go to your neighbor's house for entertainment, to listen to stories and learn customary dances and songs; they will go to the American Club for entertainment, to play tennis, grab a burger, and watch the latest movies on a big-screen TV.

At first, the decadent or detached life of the diplomats may confuse you. You'll marvel at the limited extent to which many embassy personnel interact with host country nationals, especially in comparison with your experiences. You'll ponder the efficacy and purpose of an institution seemingly isolated or out of touch with the realities of the country it purports to aid and assist. Then you'll come in from the bush one day, go to the American Club (assuming USAID has a presence and has constructed one in your country), and all that confusion will morph into envy and appreciation.

If there is an American Club at the U.S. embassy, Peace Corps volunteers are usually granted access, which, you'll come to realize, is a real gift and gracious gesture. Typically only embassy diplomats and Peace Corps staff have automatic club privileges. Everyone else must be accompanied by a paying member to use the facilities. American Clubs have snack bars (serving burgers, ice cream, and American candy), swimming pools, TV rooms with a video library and a satellite hooked up to AFRTS (an army station that broadcasts everything from network news and sports events to soap operas and prime-time favorites), and tennis courts. If you are posted to a small, rural village, far removed from all that is American and familiar, you will appreciate the luxury of the club when you come in to the capital to take care of Peace Corps business.

As for the rest of the embassy (the embassy restaurant, the money-changing desk, the commissary, the computer labs, the medical and mail services, and so on), Peace Corps volunteers are usually denied access. In smaller programs or countries, there may be a closer relationship between the embassy and the Peace Corps, in which case you may interact and have more embassy privileges. For the most part, however, don't count on being treated as a diplomat or being granted the same access to the embassy.

Part XII

Traveling Like a Pro

67

Will I have the opportunity to travel much during my two years as a volunteer?

Officially PCVs are allowed two vacation days per month—forty-eight days for two years—to use as they please. The Peace Corps imposes only a few restrictions on those vacation days, which are (1) vacation request forms must be submitted to program directors for approval; (2) vacation days must be earned before they are claimed; and (3) volunteers should refrain from vacationing during their first and last three months at post (to facilitate acculturation/integration upon arrival and wrapping-up/packing-up upon departure).

As a volunteer serving for two years in a foreign and often exotic country, however, you are guaranteed to encounter travel opportunities that conflict with the Peace Corps' policies. In those situations, think carefully before throwing caution to the wind. On the one hand, most volunteers take at least a few unofficial vacations, which we called "clando" (as in "clandestine") trips, during their time in the Peace Corps. On the other hand, if you are caught, be prepared for anything from a reprimand to an administrative separation.

Clando trips aside, you should find that opportunities to travel during your Peace Corps service are profuse. In my opinion, there is little excuse to spend two years in one country without seeing all there is to see. Take the time, plan the trips, get some folks together, and do it.

If you're thinking about traveling outside your country of service during your two years, you'll need to plan, budget, and prepare more carefully than for domestic trips, but it can easily be done. Of course, you shouldn't make your international trip one of your clando adventures—it's a surefire way to get thrown out of the Peace Corps, and it's dangerous to boot. During my second year of service,

I took three weeks of official vacation to travel through three West African countries with a group of friends. Others I knew flew to Kenya for a month, checked out South Africa, met their folks in London for Christmas, flew back to the States for a wedding, and so on. If you have the time and means, such trips are worthwhile breaks from Peace Corps life, and offer adventures and opportunities you may not encounter without leaving your country of service.

In any Peace Corps program, there are always a handful of volunteers who refrain from taking trips of any kind, preferring to stay in their villages instead. In truth, they are often better integrated, slightly more productive, and feel more at home in their local communities that most. On the other hand, they fail to attain a more holistic impression of their country of service and miss out on various cultural and social opportunities their fellow volunteers enjoy. Different strokes for different folks—it just goes to show there is no right or wrong approach to the Peace Corps experience.

68

Can I travel to other countries after my Peace Corps service is over?

Yes, you can. In fact, post–Peace Corps travel is often cited as one of the reasons people join the Peace Corps to begin with. (In their operations manual, the Peace Corps even states that travel is a "valuable adjunct to the total Volunteer experience.") When you complete your service, you will be offered the choice of receiving a Peace Corps–issued ticket back to your permanent home of record in the States or receiving the cash value of that ticket in either U.S. dollars or the local currency. Since Uncle Sam typically buys nonexcursion one-way tickets, the fares are usually worth quite a bit of money. Many RPCVs take the "cash in lieu of" (as it's often referred to in the Peace Corps) and purchase tickets to various exotic destinations around the world.

You will also receive one-third of your readjustment allowance (typically a few thousand dollars) in the form of a U.S. government treasury check upon COS'ing—an amount sufficient to finance your travels after purchasing the plane tickets with your "cash in lieu of" money. Traveling post-PC can be especially low-budget considering you will have just spent two years perfecting the art of shoestring living in your village. Also, as a newly COS'ed volunteer, you can plug into the PCV network wherever you travel, staying in rest houses and PCVs' homes, gaining unique insights into other countries and forging new friendships along the way.

Many wonder why some COS'ing volunteers take the PC-issued return ticket home and forgo the chance to jet around the world as only an RPCV can. There are several reasons. Many volunteers, as they approach their COS date, begin to appreciate the magnitude of the challenges that lie ahead of them in terms of readjustment to life in the States. Knowing that they face indefinite unemployment and a renewed dependence on Mom and Dad, if even for a month or two, can be incredibly depressing. In that state of mind, jetting around the world may seem like delaying the inevitable and perhaps worsening it by burning through your readjustment allowance before you really need it.

Others are comfortable with the thought of moving back home but are anxious to start their job search or prepare for graduate school. Some are simply fed up with living like bohemians and find no appeal in the thought of backpacking around, living like a grub for another six months. They figure they've spent two years living an adventurous, tumultuous, unpredictable life, and welcome the opportunity to construct a more stable or structured life back in the States.

69

Will I be issued a diplomatic passport?

No, you will not be issued a diplomatic (aka "black") passport. You will, however, have a special note on the inside of your passport indicating that you are a Peace Corps volunteer, which helps distinguish you from a tourist and often results in a certain degree of preferential treatment (particularly when dealing with customs officials, border crossings, and local police).

The difference between a regular U.S. passport, which Peace Corps volunteers are issued, and a diplomatic one is substantial. Carriers of diplomatic passports are essentially "above the law." They cannot be prosecuted by local officials for breaching local (national) laws. They are granted immunities and embassy privileges that other Americans overseas are denied.

Aside from your passport, however, you will be issued an official Peace Corps identification card once you swear in as a volunteer. Your Peace Corps ID may not wield as much power as a passport, but it will certainly wield as much influence in many parts of the world. While it's not practical to carry your passport with you at all times during your Peace Corps service (in fact, it's best to store it in the Peace Corps safe), you should carry your Peace Corps ID religiously. Most officials in countries where the Peace Corps works are familiar with the organization and its structure. As such, your ID card will suffice during routine stops, checks, or crossings.

Part XIII

Post–Peace Corps

70

How hard is readjusting to life back in the States?

If you are thinking of joining the Peace Corps, or you have already been accepted and are waiting to leave, readjustment to life in the States after your service is probably the last thing on your mind. In fact, if someone asked you about it, you'd probably respond by asking, "What is there to readjust to?" Well, for those of you with the foresight to wonder and worry about this issue, I'll address it briefly now.

In short, readjustment is as difficult as, if not more difficult than, adjusting to life overseas. Once you have spent two years in the Peace Corps, you have adapted both externally and internally. You have changed the way you think, perceive, react, converse, analyze, expect, dream, live, digest, and learn. You have modified your behavior to adapt to an extreme circumstance—so much so that the extreme becomes mundane, and you no longer feel alienated from a culture so distant from the one you left behind in the States.

When your two years are up and you come back home, the vastness and breadth of your experience and the ways in which it affected you become glaringly obvious. What you once thought would be easy and effortless is suddenly as impossible and intimidating as moving overseas once was—only worse because you didn't expect it. Even though "reverse culture shock" is touched on during your COS conference, and stories of readjustment hell are abundant in the overseas volunteer community, you won't appreciate the challenges that lie ahead of you until you reach the States.

It's not just about reacclimating to the weather, the food, the fast pace of life, and the highly structured social environment. It's about realizing that your life is suddenly in your own hands again. Two years in the Peace Corps' cradling arm, though seemingly invisible at times during your service, will have spoiled you. And when that arm jettisons you out toward the glass and concrete of mainstream U.S.A., you'll inevitably feel disoriented.

Most RPCVs, having joined the Peace Corps soon after graduating from college, return to the States without a job or a place to live. As such, the rigors of emotional readjustment are compounded by the need for physical and financial readjustment. Others, however, manage to line up grad school or employment offers before they COS. For these lucky few, all of the mental and emotional hurdles discussed here apply but are mitigated somewhat by the structure that awaits them. Regardless of an RPCV's level of preparedness, the nature of transitioning back to life in the States requires certain adjustments that simply can't be avoided: acknowledging that your own culture feels somewhat alien to you; shifting perspective to accommodate the wealth and waste of American society; changing mental gears to join the breakneck pace of the developed world; and so on.

For the typical RPCV (that is, one who returns to the States unsure of the next step), readjustment seems to follow a pattern. Stage one starts with elation as you embrace your family and plop on the sofa to bask in being "home." After spending a few weeks telling stories and visiting old friends, stage two sets in: confusion with a dash of depression. You realize you've visited everyone, told your best stories, spent your readjustment allowance, and have begun to wear out the welcome mat at your parents' house. You also realize that, after catching up with friends, they went to work the next day, while you plopped on the couch again to watch more TV.

Enter stage three: panic. You suddenly look around and realize that to truly reestablish yourself as a contributing member of society, you have to get a job. You need money, a place to live, a means of transport, and, most importantly, a purpose in life. Unfortunately not one of those is easy to come by. In fact, they require kicking, screaming, scrambling, and competing with other folks—a far cry from the requirements of everyday life back in your Peace Corps village. You feel at once anxious and overwhelmed, and you wonder how you could have ever thought coming home would be easy.

The remaining stages are similar to any you'd experience if you were recently graduating from college or switching jobs. They involve all the frustration, despair, elation, and anxiety that are normally associated with job searching. Each small step you take at this point brings you closer and closer to complete readjustment. In the end, when you are moved into your own apartment, you are gainfully employed, your credit cards are under control, and you no longer freak out in grocery stores or mega-malls, you'll feel a deep satisfaction at what you've accomplished. You will have come full circle, but that circle will encompass an experience more personal and enriching than most can comprehend.

71

Does the Peace Corps look good on a resume? Will it help me get into graduate school?

As difficult as returning to the States may be, one thing you can count on to lessen the blow and boost your spirits is praise and admiration from everyone who knows or discovers that you are an RPCV. No matter how you feel about the Peace Corps based on your personal experiences overseas, you'll most likely discover that the majority of Americans view the organization in a straightforward, overwhelmingly positive light. The more you speak to them of the Peace Corps' complexities and realities, the more you confirm their impression of the Peace Corps as something few Americans can endure.

Needless to say, the Peace Corps looks great on a resume and provides a nice stepping stone for any number of career paths you may decide to follow. Oftentimes your program and project accomplishments won't even matter—potential employers will see that you served in the Peace Corps and conclude that you are dependable, determined, confident, adaptable, resourceful, and personable. If your overseas experience actually fits the requirements of the position for which you are applying, the stepping stone will take you even closer to, and perhaps directly to, a new job. I've never heard an RPCV speak of the Peace Corps as a detriment to his or her resume.

Another way that the Peace Corps can help land you a job is through an extensive RPCV network. Once you start job searching, you'll quickly realize that RPCVs are everywhere—the public sector, the private sector, NGOs, and so on. With the help of the Peace Corps' Returned Volunteer Services Office and the myriad of RPCV websites and online social networks, you can tap into the returned volunteer community to expand and expedite your job search (see appendix G).

Your Peace Corps experience puts you head and shoulders over other applicants for graduate school as well, for all the reasons I cited earlier. You will stand out as an individual who has learned about the world in a way few others have—a valuable contribution to any course of study. You will have demonstrated that you have personality traits necessary to tackle graduate programs with commitment and determination. You will have proven that you possess an acute ability to absorb, process, learn, solve problems creatively, and thrive under adverse and challenging conditions—something few graduate admissions offices fail to appreciate.

In addition, Peace Corps has established cooperative relationships with over fifty graduate schools to offer Master's International programs to those interested in pursuing advanced degrees in conjunction with their Peace Corps service. As a Master's International student, you can receive credit for your two years overseas and apply that credit toward any number of graduate programs in fields as varied as business, public health and nutrition, and forestry. Typically students complete one to two years of graduate study at a participating institution, then head overseas to begin their Peace Corps assignments. At the end of the program, you come out with an advanced degree and two years of overseas work experience—an unbeatable combination and, in many cases, a prerequisite for career-track jobs in the international arena. For more information on the Master's International program, refer to appendix E.

72

What is "noncompetitive eligibility" and what can it do for me?

Noncompetitive eligibility (NCE) gives you special hiring consideration for federal government jobs. It identifies you as an "insider," on par with current federal employees in the eyes of human resource departments and the Office of Personnel Management (OPM). As such, NCE qualifies you for positions that may be closed to the general public, virtually doubling the number of job opportunities available to you. It also exempts you from having to be the best-qualified candidate for a given job; rather you are only required to meet the minimum qualifications as specified in a vacancy announcement. NCE allows you to be more proactive in your federal job search by opening more doors and eliminating a few layers of bureaucracy. All RPCVs are granted NCE for one year from their COS date. Under certain circumstances, and with prior approval, extensions may be granted.

If you work for the federal government after the Peace Corps, your volunteer service will help in other ways too. If your new duties and responsibilities directly relate to your Peace Corps experience, you may qualify for a higher grade or step, translating to increased pay. You will have two years' credit toward retirement and vacation hours earned per pay period (though you must buy into the system to receive this credit; a human resources office in any federal agency can explain this procedure to you). You will also have access to an astonishing network of RPCVs in the federal system, which can help advance your career in more subtle ways.

If you have questions about NCE and the ways it can be used to your advantage, don't hesitate to contact the Returned Volunteer Services Office at the Peace Corps and speak with a career counselor. It's a unique and valuable perk; don't let it go to waste!

73

Can I bring my Peace Corps pet back to the States with me?

Yes, but it could take more time and money to send ol' Spot back to Cleveland than you may think. Understanding that some people get really attached to their pets, I'll try not to discourage the practice of bringing them back to the States. But think hard about it before jumping in with both feet. Remember that there are plenty of homeless pets in the States that are just begging to be adopted, and that any pet born and bred overseas may suffer before acclimating to a more restrictive life in the States. Peace Corps pets generally have free rein at volunteers' posts—they know no leash laws, city sidewalks, busy streets, small yards, animal pounds, or doghouses—quite a difference from pet life in this country, unless you happen to live on a ranch in Wyoming.

If you are intent on bringing a pet back with you, you'll need to contact the Ministry of Agriculture (or equivalent) to purchase a "pet export license." Cost will vary from country to country, as will processing time. You'll also need to take your pet to a U.S.-certified veterinarian (the embassy can you provide you with a list) and have the animal examined and vaccinated. If the veterinarian is not U.S. certified, your pet's health records will not be admitted by custom officials in the States. Last of all, contact the airline and inquire about costs and regulations associated with pet transport. Volunteers I spoke with who went through this process mentioned that airports in several countries prohibit the loading of animals onto planes when the tarmac is over eighty degrees Fahrenheit. On dry season days, which constitute half the year in much of the developing world, the tarmac can get even hotter than that, so keep those kinds of rules in mind when booking your flight.

74

Would you go back and do the Peace Corps all over again?

"I would do it with a few years of professional experience under my belt so I would have more to offer my village. And I'd have different expectations going in, more realistic. Also, a third year would have been more effective."
—Naomi Roots, Environmental Education RPCV, Nicaragua, 2005–2007

"I would have finished my master's first and gotten some work experience before joining."
—RPCV, Bolivia, 2006–2008

"I would do it again after retirement, or as a married couple. And I'd do it in a completely different country, for a new experience. I think it's a great program."
—Melissa Salgado, CED RPCV, Panama, 2005–2007

"Yes! I'd do it again if I had to repeat my life story. And I'd like to do it again after retirement."
—Colleen Duffy, Agricultural Marketing RPCV, Guatemala, 2003–2005

"No, not if the aim were solely to do development work. If the aim were to travel and learn new languages and cultures, then yes."
—RPCV, Dominican Republic, 2005–2007

"During the first six months of my service, I was considered the most likely to terminate early. But at my COS conference two years later, I was voted most likely to do Peace Corps again. And I did a third year."
—Amy Heasley, TEFL RPCV, Ukraine, 2004–2007

"Yes, but only married. As a couple, PC treats you so much differently. Unmarried PCVs under thirty get treated as children; married ones get immediate respect. PC also checks up on them less, and a higher level of responsibility is assumed. Lastly, two incomes, one rent, two settling-in allowances, one house to furnish, and—the biggie—having someone from home there to complain, gossip, etc., with."
    —RPCV, Dominican Republic 2005–2006

"Absolutely. But there wouldn't be the same excitement and intensity as the first time."
    —Kathy Kacen, TEFL RPCV, Armenia, 2002–2005

"This question is repeatedly asked when I discuss Peace Corps. I do not regret doing Peace Corps. Would I do it again? No. I believe that a lot of the problems I faced were compounded by the Peace Corps, but were due to the adjustment issues I had while living in Romania. The country itself is harsh."
    —RPCV, Romania, 2005–2007

"Yes . . . but I would have held out for a placement in education instead of filling the summer quota simply because I was ready to leave."
    —RPCV, Dominican Republic, 2000–2002

"Yes. It wasn't exactly the experience that I expected, but I am grateful to have met the people in South Africa that I did and would say my two years there were the most meaningful years of my life thus far. I believe I had a strong impact on the lives of several South Africans as well."
    —RPCV, South Africa, 2005–2007

"Absolutely. No matter what you read or what people tell you, it will be different from what you expect. I feel like every aspect of it is different for each person and you never know what it is going to be like until you are in it."
    —RPCV, Macedonia, 2004–2006

"If it were up to me, I'd still be there right now!"
    —Steve Ripes, Math and Science Education RPCV, Cameroon, 2002–2005

Appendices

Appendix A

Peace Corps General Facts

The Mission of the Peace Corps
To help the people of interested countries in meeting their need for trained men and women. To help promote a better understanding of Americans on the part of the peoples served. To help promote a better understanding of other peoples on the part of Americans.

History
Peace Corps Officially Established: March 1, 1961
Total Number of Volunteers and Trainees to Date: 190,000
Total Number of Countries Served: 139

Volunteers
Current Number of Volunteers and Trainees: 8,079

Gender:	59% female, 41% male
Marital Status:	93% single, 7% married
Minorities:	17% of Peace Corps volunteers
Average Age:	27 years old
Volunteers over 50:	5% of Peace Corps volunteers
Oldest Volunteer:	80 years old
Education:	11% graduate studies/degrees
	95% undergraduate degrees

Countries
Current Number of Countries Served: 74

FY '08 Budget: $330.8 million

Recruitment Toll-Free Number: (800) 424-8580

Website: www.peacecorps.gov

Revised 9/07

Appendix B

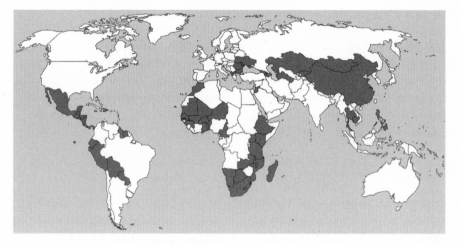

© MAGELLAN Geographix℠Santa Barbara, CA (800) 929-4MAP   Robinson Projection

Peace Corps Country Map

AFRICA
Benin, Botswana, Burkina Faso, Cameroon, Cape Verde, Ethiopia, The Gambia, Ghana, Guinea, Kenya, Lesotho, Madagascar, Malawi, Mali, Mauritania, Mozambique, Namibia, Niger, Senegal, South Africa, Swaziland, Tanzania, Togo, Uganda, Zambia

INTER-AMERICA AND THE CARIBBEAN
Antigua/Barbuda, Belize, Bolivia, Costa Rica, Dominica, Dominican Republic, Ecuador, El Salvador, Grenada & Carriacou, Guatemala, Guyana, Honduras, Jamaica, Mexico, Nicaragua, Panama, Paraguay, Peru, St. Kitts and Nevis, St. Lucia, St. Vincent/Grenadines, Suriname

CENTRAL AND EAST ASIA
Cambodia, China, Kazakhstan, Kyrgyz Republic, Mongolia, Philippines, Thailand, Turkmenistan

EUROPE AND THE MEDITERRANEAN
Albania, Armenia, Azerbaijan, Bulgaria, Georgia, Jordan, Macedonia, Moldova, Morocco, Romania, Ukraine

PACIFIC ISLANDS
Federated States of Micronesia, Fiji, Kiribati, Republic of Palau, Samoa, Tonga, Vanuatu

Appendix C

Peace Corps Programs Overview

The following is a list of Peace Corps Programs and a general overview of each program. Remember, Peace Corps service is possible even if you don't "fit" exactly into these categories. Liberal arts majors and "generalists" are encouraged to apply. Contact a Peace Corps recruiter at (800) 424-8580 to discuss how your educational and/or work experiences apply to these programs, and to request more information on specific requirements and relevant experience.

EDUCATION AND YOUTH AND COMMUNITY DEVELOPMENT

Primary Education Teacher Training
Volunteers provide formal and informal training and support to elementary school teachers and occasionally provide classroom instruction.

Secondary Education English Teaching
Volunteers teach conversational English, English as a foreign language, or content-based English in middle and high schools.

Secondary Education Math or Science Teaching
Volunteers in math teach basic concepts, including remedial math, geometry, algebra, statistics, probability, and calculus. Volunteers in science teach general science, biology, chemistry, and physics.

Secondary Education English Teacher Training
Teacher trainers work with new and experienced English teachers, training students teachers at teachers' colleges or providing in-service training to experienced teachers in current

methodologies, subject content, and resource development.

Special Education Teacher Training
Volunteers work with education offices, schools, and local teachers, focusing on methodology, individualized instruction, classroom management, and resource development for teachers of students with special needs.

University English Teaching
Volunteers work with university-level students who need enhanced English language skills to make use of academic and technical resources published in English in their study of languages, literature, business, medicine, engineering, or other fields.

Construction and Skilled Trades Education
Volunteers teach vocational education in schools, technical institutes, and training centers. They also work with communities and local governments to facilitate the construction of schools, health centers, markets, and other projects while transferring their skills to tradespeople and students in their communities.

Youth Development
Volunteers work with at-risk youth ages 10 to 25, helping communities develop programs to assist young people.

Community Development
Volunteers coordinate with other Peace Corps projects by conducting community outreach and needs assessments.

HEALTH AND HIV/AIDS

Health Extension
Volunteers raise awareness in communities about the need for health education.

Public Health Education
Volunteers teach public health in classrooms and model methodologies and subjects for primary and secondary school teachers. Volunteers also work in local health clinics to develop health education and outreach programs.

Water and Sanitation Extension
Volunteers serve in a broad range of projects, including organizing and mobilizing communities to provide health and hygiene education; tapping springs, constructing wells, and building latrines; improving potable water storage facilities; and doing community outreach.

AGRICULTURE

Agriculture and Forestry Extension
Volunteers' projects include establishing and maintaining soil- and water-conservation structures and practices; fruit tree production; live fences; fish cultivation; raising trees in small nurseries, and other projects.

Applied Agricultural Science
Volunteers encourage sustainable crop production through promotion of organic-farming techniques and better farm management.

Farm Management and Agribusiness
Volunteers teach basic business practices such as marketing and credit price determination; work on crop and livestock production and preservation; assist in organizing of local farmers; and identify market structures and channels.

Animal Husbandry
Volunteers work to enhance farm families' nutrition and household income through improved livestock management techniques. Activities include projects such as vegetable gardening, range management, and beekeeping.

ENVIRONMENT

Environmental Education or Awareness
Volunteers assist communities where environmental issues are in conflict with basic needs for farming and income generation. Activities include teaching in elementary and secondary schools; organizing environmental groups; and development of ecotourism and other income-generating activities for communities living near protected areas.

Forestry
Volunteers help communities conserve natural resources by working on projects such as soil conservation; watershed management and flood control; production of sustainable fuels; and improvement of agroforestry practices such as fruit production.

Protected-Areas Management

Volunteers provide technical assistance and training in natural resource conservation, generally in close affiliation with national parks or other reserves.

Environmental and Water Resources Engineering

Volunteers work with local governments and communities to improve water and sanitation facilities.

BUSINESS DEVLOPMENT

Business Advising

Volunteers work in a variety of settings, assisting both private and public businesses, local and regional governments, nonprofit organizations, women's and youth groups, and educational institutions.

Business Development

Volunteers consult with businesses and conduct seminars on starting a business, strategic planning, marketing, merchandising, organizational development, and tourism development.

Nongovernmental Organization Development

Volunteers work with local, national, or international nongovernmental organizations (NGOs) that deal with youth, social services, health services, HIV/AIDS prevention, small business development, or the environment.

BUSINESS DEVELOPMENT AND INFORMATION TECHNOLOGY

Urban and Regional Planning

Volunteers work with municipalities and communities, as well as with regional or national governments. Projects include assessing the impact of planned activities or economic and environmental development on communities, and planning infrastructure for primary and secondary cities.

Information Technology

Volunteers provide technical training and support to school systems, health ministries, municipal government offices, and nongovernmental organizations. Projects include teaching computer skills and data processing, helping to develop regional databases, and implementing networks for business and government offices.

Appendix D

Medical Information for Applicants

In order to make sure that Peace Corps is able to protect the health and safety of its volunteers overseas, Peace Corps requires that an applicant have the physical and mental capacity, with or without a medical accommodation, to perform the essential functions of a volunteer for a full tour of duty without unreasonable disruption due to health problems. Peace Corps may not be able to accommodate certain medical or psychiatric conditions.

Stable conditions as well as medication regimes (both medical and psychiatric) can be appropriate for Peace Corps service and are considered during the preservice evaluation. Recent changes in these conditions or medication regimes (both medical and psychiatric) are evaluated on an individual basis and may require a period of proven stability prior to Peace Corps service.

Because of the nature of the countries in which Peace Corps serves, the scope of medical care available in those countries, and the conditions under which volunteers live and work, the Peace Corps may not be able to accommodate certain medical or psychiatric conditions.

After individually assessing each applicant, Peace Corps is typically *unable* to reasonably accommodate applicants with the conditions below. This list may not include all conditions:

Addison's Disease

Allergic Reaction, life-threatening

Amyotrophic Lateral Sclerosis (Lou Gehrig's Disease)

Aneurysm, inoperable

Asthma, severe

Chronic Obstructive Pulmonary Disease (COPD)

Cancer (recent treatment for cancer or cancer with metastasis)

Cardiac Arrhythmias, symptomatic

Cystic Fibrosis

Complex health conditions with multiple diagnoses

Conditions requiring blood thinner medication

Conditions requiring oral or injectable steroids

Connective Tissue Disorders

Coronary Artery Disease

Crohn's Disease

Diabetes with any complications

Diverticulitis

Endocarditis

Esophageal Varices

Glomerulonephritis, chronic

Heart Conditions, chronic

Heart Failure

Hematological Disorder, chronic

Hemophilia

Hepatitis, chronic

Human Immunodeficiency Virus (HIV)

Inflammatory Bowel Disease

Irreversible Lung Disease (emphysema)

Iritis, chronic

Kidney Stones, recurrent

Major Depression, recurrent

Muscular Dystrophy

Multiple Sclerosis (no exacerbation or new symptoms for a minimum of 10 years)

Myasthenia Gravis

Narcolepsy (poorly controlled)

Obstructive Sleep Apnea (with or without C-PAP machine)

Optic Neuritis, recurrent

Osteoporosis (with history or high risk for stress fractures)

Pancreatitis, chronic

Parkinson's Disease

Psychosis

Psychiatric Hospitalization (within a year)

Pyelonephritis, chronic

Reiter's Syndrome, chronic

Rheumatoid Arthritis

Sarcoidosis

Schizophrenia

Thromobophlebitis, recurrent

Ulcerative Colitis

Uveitis, chronic

Ventricular Shunt (for hydrocephalus)

If an applicant is currently dealing with any of the following conditions, his/her invitation to the Peace Corps will be deferred until the condition is resolved. The length of the deferral period varies according to the individual case.

Abnormal Pap Smear requiring current treatment

Allergies requiring desensitization injections

Anemia (cause must be identified)

Cataracts requiring surgery

Endometriosis

Inguinal Hernia

Internal Hemorrhoids

Kidney or Bladder Infections

Orthodontic Braces (excluding bite-plate)

Ovarian Cyst

Uterine Fibroids (symptomatic)

Cancer (3 years cancer-free; no deferral for most skin cancers and carcinoma-in-situ)

Coronary artery bypass surgery or angioplasty (6 months symptom-free, no medications, normal stress test)

Cystic Acne—Accutane treatment (2 months after completion of therapy)

Gastritis, Esophagitis, Peptic, or Duodenal Ulcer (minimum of 6 months well controlled, nonsmoker)

Glaucoma (3 months well controlled with medications or 6 months after surgical treatment)

Herniated Disc (minimum of 2 years symptom free)

Herpes Keratitis, eye (2 years inactive)

High Blood Pressure (3 months well controlled under treatment; weight within medically recommended range)

Joint or Back Disorders must be stable or mild; weight within medically recommended range

Joint Replacement (hip, knee, shoulder) or arthroscopy—1 year

Ligament Reconstruction (knee, ankle, shoulder) or arthroscopy—1 year

Myocardial Infarction (heart attack)—12 months symptom free, not on medication, normal stress test

Seizure Disorder—minimum of 1 year seizure free

Stroke—2 years symptom free, not on medication

Some Psychological Conditions

Alcoholism, Substance Addiction—minimum of 3 years for alcoholism, minimum of 5 years for substance abuse

Note that you cannot be invited to a Peace Corps program until you have completed the medical review process. Please complete your evaluations as quickly as possible.

Receipt of a medical and dental clearance is based on your medical and dental status at that time. If, after your clearance, you become ill, undergo surgery, add to or change medications, undergo therapy or treatment, or develop any condition for which you seek medical assistance; please notify [Peace Corps] immediately. Any significant change in your health status may impact your medical/dental clearance. Failure to disclose such information may seriously affect your health overseas, as well as your status as a Peace Corps trainee/volunteer. For further information, call the Office of Medical Services at (800) 424-8580, ext. 1500, from 10:00 A.M. to 4:00 P.M., Monday through Friday (Eastern Time).

Revised 01/08

Appendix E

Peace Corps Master's International Program

The Master's International program incorporates Peace Corps service into a master's degree program at universities across the United States. As Master's International participants, students spend one to two years completing course work on campus. Afterward, they serve overseas in the Peace Corps for 27 months, for which they receive academic credit. Generally, students then return to the university for one semester to complete degree requirements.

For more information:

Website: www.peacecorps.gov/masters

Email: mastersinternational@peacecorps.gov

Phone: (202) 692-1812 or (800) 424-8580, ext. 1812

The universities participating in the program in various fields are listed as follows:

AGRICULTURE AND AGRIBUSINESS

Arizona State University—Mesa

Clemson University—SC

Colorado State University—
Fort Collins

Cornell University—Ithaca, NY

Michigan State University—
East Lansing

North Carolina Agricultural and
Technical State University—
Greensboro

Texas A&M University—
College Station

Texas Tech University—Lubbock

University of California—Davis

University of Georgia—Athens

University of Nebraska—Lincoln

University of Wisconsin—Madison

Washington State University—Pullman

BUSINESS, ECONOMICS, COMMUNITY DEVELOPMENT, URBAN PLANNING, YOUTH DEVELOPMENT

Florida State University—Tallahassee

George Mason University—Fairfax, VA

Illinois State University—Normal

Monterey Institute of International
Studies—CA

School for International Training—
Brattleboro, VT

Southern New Hampshire
University—Manchester

University of Alaska—Fairbanks

University of Cincinnati—OH

University of Montana—Missoula

University of South Florida—Tampa

University of the Pacific—
Stockton, CA

University of Wisconsin—Madison

Virginia Polytechnic Institute and
State University—Blacksburg

ENVIRONMENT, FORESTRY, NATURAL RESOURCES, ENGINEERING

Bard College—Annandale-on-Hudson, NY

Clemson University—SC

Colorado State University—Fort Collins

Cornell University—Ithaca, NY

Florida International University—Miami

Michigan State University—East Lansing

Michigan Technological University—Houghton

Northern Arizona University—Flagstaff

North Carolina State University—Raleigh

Texas A&M University—College Station

Texas Tech University—Lubbock

University of Alaska—Fairbanks

University of Cincinnati—OH

University of Colorado—Denver

University of Georgia—Athens

University of Maryland—College Park

University of Minnesota—St. Paul

University of Montana—Missoula

University of Washington—Seattle

University of Wisconsin—Madison

University of Wisconsin—Stevens Point

Washington State University—Pullman

EDUCATION (e.g., MATH, SCIENCE, ENGLISH), WRITING, ENGLISH AS A SECOND LANGUAGE

American University—Washington, D.C.

Appalachian State University—Boone, NC

California State University—Sacramento

Clemson University—SC

Colorado State University—Fort Collins

Florida State University—Tallahassee

George Mason University—Fairfax, VA

Georgia State University—Atlanta

Humboldt State University—Arcata, CA

Michigan Technological University—Houghton

Monterey Institute of International Studies—CA

North Carolina Agricultural and Technical State University—Greensboro

Saint Michael's College—Colchester, VT

School for International Training—Brattleboro, VT

Texas Tech University—Lubbock

University of Maryland—Baltimore Country

University of Nevada—Las Vegas

ADMINISTRATION, INTERNATIONAL STUDIES, PUBLIC POLICY, POLITICAL SCIENCE, SOCIOLOGY

Cornell University—Ithaca, NY

George Mason University—Fairfax, VA

Georgia State University—Atlanta

Illinois State University—Normal

Monterey Institute of International Studies—CA

Oklahoma State University—Stillwater

Rutgers, State University of New Jersey—Camden

School for International Training—Brattleboro, VT

University of Cincinnati—OH

Univerity of Denver—CO

University of the Pacific—Stockton, CA

University of Washington—Seattle

University of Wyoming—Laramie

Virginia Polytechnic Institute and State University—Blacksburg

Western Michigan University—Kalamazoo

PUBLIC HEALTH, INTERNATIONAL HEALTH, NURSING, NUTRITION

Boston University—Massachusetts

Colorado State University—Fort Collins

Cornell University—Ithaca, NY

Emory University—Atlanta, GA

George Mason University—Fairfax, VA

George Washington University—Washington, D.C.

Johns Hopkins University—Baltimore, MD

Loma Linda University—CA

Tulane University—New Orleans, LA

University of Alabama—Birmingham

University of South Florida—Tampa

University of Washington—Seattle

Appendix F

Peace Corps Regional Offices

Atlanta Region
(AL, FL, GA, MS, PR, SC, TN, USVI)
100 Alabama Street
Building 1924, Suite 2R70
Atlanta, GA 30303
(404) 562-3456
Fax: (404) 562-3455
atlinfo@peacecorps.gov

Boston Region
(MA, ME, NH, RI, VT)
Tip O'Neill Federal Building
10 Causeway Street
Suite 450
Boston, MA 02222
(617) 565-5555
Fax: (617) 565-5539
boston@peacecorps.gov

Chicago Region
(IL, IN, KY, MI, MO, OH)
55 West Monroe Street
Suite 450
Chicago, IL 60603
(312) 353-4990
Fax: (312) 353-4192
chicago@peacecorps.gov

Dallas Region
(AR, LA, NM, OK, TX)
1100 Commerce Street
Suite 427
Dallas, TX 75242
(214) 253-5400
Fax: (214) 253-5401
dallas@peacecorps.gov

Denver Region
(CO, KS, NE, UT, WY)
1999 Broadway
Suite 2205
Denver, CO 80202
(303) 844-7020
Fax: (303) 844-7010
denver@peacecorps.gov

Los Angeles Region
(AZ, Southern CA)
2361 Rosecrans Avenue
Suite 155
El Segundo, CA 90245
(310) 356-1100
Fax: (310) 356-1125
lainfo@peacecorps.gov

Minneapolis Region
(IA, MN, ND, SD, WI)
330 Second Avenue South
Suite 420
Minneapolis, MN 55401
(612) 348-1480
Fax: (612) 348-1474
minneapolis@peacecorps.gov

New York Region
(CT, NJ, NY, PA)
201 Varick Street
Suite 1025
New York, NY 10014
(212) 352-5440
Fax: (212) 352-5441
nyinfo@peacecorps.gov

San Francisco Region
(Northern CA, HI, NV)
1301 Clay Street
Suite 620N
Oakland, CA 94612
(510) 452-8444
Fax: (510) 452-8441
sfinfo@peacecorps.gov

Seattle Region
(AK, ID, MT, OR, WA)
1601 Fifth Avenue
Suite 605
Seattle, WA 98101
(206) 553-5490
Fax: (206) 553-2343
seattle@peacecorps.gov

Washington, D.C. Region
(DC, DE, MD, NC, VA, WV)
1525 Wilson Boulevard
Suite 100
Arlington, VA 22209
(202) 692-1040
Fax: (202) 692-1065
dcinfo@peacecorps.gov

Revised 10/07

Appendix G

Peace Corps Information Online

www.peacecorps.gov
Peace Corps' official website. Includes program-specific information, "how to apply" section, online registration and application, frequently asked questions, returned volunteer section, contact information, diversity discussion, and much more.

www.rpcv.org
National Peace Corps Association (NPCA) website. Aimed at the RPCV community, but provides links to other PC-related organizations, email address search capabilities (to find RPCVs from specific countries), and more.

**www.rpcv.org/pages/groups
.cfm?category=2**
Lists over 130 Peace Corps alumni groups affiliated with the NPCA. Most of the groups are either community-based (for example, the Louisiana or Cincinnati group) or are identified by country of Peace Corps service (called "Friends of" groups). In addition, some networks are based on shared interests. In addition to promoting global education and supporting overseas development projects, the groups often work with Peace Corps recruiting offices to support recently returned PCVs and sponsor forums for information and issue discussions.

http://peacecorpsonline.org
An "independent news forum" for everything and anything related to the Peace Corps. Includes current and past news items, bulletin boards, web links, featured stories, annual reports, official documents, and much more.

www.peacecorpsjournals.com
A worldwide Peace Corps blog directory, with pull-down menus to access blogs that focus on everything from regional and geographic areas to Peace Corps writers, women volunteers, minorities, and more.

www.peacecorpswiki.org
Peace Corps Wiki is a collaborative project whose goal is to create a free, interactive, and up-to-date source of information about serving as a volunteer with the U.S. Peace Corps. Anyone is welcome to edit, add, or change any entry, or start a new one. So far there are a total of 2,615 pages that have been written and edited by RPCVs, PCVs, and friends of Peace Corps from around the world. The site includes helpful information for prospective PCVs, including the entire *Peace Corps Manual*, detailing the agency's rules and regulations governing volunteers in the field.

**www.peacecorps.gov/news/
resources/stats/pdf/schools2008.pdf**
This page of the official Peace Corps
website lists the colleges and universities that produced the most Peace
Corps Volunteers in 2007.

**www.peacecorps.gov/
minisite/50plus/index.cfm**
Peace Corp's "mini-site" dedicated to
issues affecting or pertaining to older
volunteers. Includes good information
on health and insurance, finance, and
medical clearance, as well as multimedia clips from current and returned
PCVs in the 50+ age bracket.

www.lgbrpcv.org/articles.htm
A wealth of insight and articles on the
lesbian, gay, bisexual, and transgender
Peace Corps experience, including a
section aimed at applicants.

**www.minoritypca.org/PCStories
.html**
The Minority Peace Corps Association's website, which includes a host
of stories from PCV minorities and
volunteers of color detailing their
experiences, perspectives, advice, and
insights.

**http://dir.groups.yahoo.com/dir/
Cultures___Community/Issues_
and_Causes/Community_Service_
and_Volunteerism/Peace_Corps**
Yahoo directory of Peace Corps-
related discussion groups centered on
the organization, countries of service,
alumni groups, applicant Q&A forums,
and so on.

www.peacecorpswriters.org
An interesting site that features books
written by RPCVs—many of which
center on their experiences from the
field.

www.peacegallery.org
A collection of Peace Corps photos,
pictures, and stories from around the
world. These are pictures taken by
PCVs (rather than the polished photos
from PC-contracted professionals).

Appendix H

Vegetarian Questionnaire

During the application process for Peace Corps service, you indicated that you are a vegetarian. In order to be healthy and safe during your service, it is our responsibility to advise you on appropriate expectations for serving as a vegetarian. While practicing vegetarianism does not mean that you cannot serve successfully as a volunteer, we would like to be certain that you have considered the various challenges to maintaining a vegetarian diet in many of the countries where Peace Corps volunteers serve. Please keep the following points in mind when considering how to maintain your vegetarian diet overseas:

1. The availability of vegetables, grains, fruits, and other food items essential to a vegetarian diet varies greatly among Peace Corps countries. While we are not asking you to change who you are, we do encourage you to be flexible about your dietary preferences in order to best meet the challenges of Peace Corps service.

2. Integrating into your community may require you to participate in cultural events that include eating meat and a variety of foods that may be unfamiliar to you. Furthermore, protein intake through meat may be necessary in order for you to stay healthy. Please note that Peace Corps will send volunteers home for medical reasons if they show signs of malnutrition.

3. Travel information intended for tourists that include vegetarian recommendations does not apply to Peace Corps service. You will most likely live in a community that is remote and/or rural and has little in common with high-traffic tourist areas.

Over the years, many vegetarians have served successfully as volunteers. While some have found adequate food items in the country's diet, many more have had to adjust their diets in order to remain healthy and maintain good relations within their communities. Since Peace Corps cannot guarantee you an assignment that will enable you to maintain your dietary preferences, we ask that you consider how you will handle serving in a country where your vegetarian diet could pose health or cross-cultural challenges. Below you will find several questions and scenarios describing situations that may arise in Peace Corps countries worldwide.

First, please describe your vegetarian diet and your reasons for being a vegetarian. Please answer the following questions using the given scenarios to inform your responses.

Scenario 1: Wednesday is market day in your village, and you are looking forward to preparing dishes in your kitchen that are familiar to you. Since your arrival, most of your meals have been with other families and have been cooked in some sort of meat broth or have included chunks of meat served with a side of white rice or boiled manioc. You wander through the market and greet the women who are crouched over small portions of small dried fish, hot peppers, and corn meal. The only vegetables you see are a few small onions.

Question 1: Have you ever had to modify your vegetarian diet because the types of food you prefer were not available? If so, please describe how you adjusted.

Scenario 2: After living with a host family for three months of training, you arrive at your rural site to find a weekly market with a limited selection of vegetables. You are very pleased to see that you have access to select vegetables and do not see any reason to make the four-hour trip to a neighboring city each week just to buy a wider variety. After a few months at site, you begin to experience headaches quite frequently, intense stomach pains, and are bruising easily. The protein powder your mom was going to send you in the mail never arrived. The symptoms become more intense, so you finally decide to seek medical attention at the Peace Corps office in the capital. You meet with the Peace Corps medical officer (PCMO) who diagnoses you with both iron and protein deficiencies. The PCMO requests that you begin eating meat, eggs, dairy, and different vegetables to improve your health situation and avoid future health concerns. You are recommended to stay under observation in the capital for a few days until your condition has noticeably improved, and you have arranged an appropriate nutrition plan to adequately follow at site.

Question 2: In what ways are you willing to adjust your diet in order to remain healthy throughout your twenty-seven months of Peace Corps service?

Scenario 3: After an exhausting sixteen-hour journey, you arrive in-country. Shortly thereafter, you and your luggage are delivered to your host family. To celebrate your arrival in their country and home, your host family prepares a traditional, festive meal. One of the few phrases you know how to say in the local language is "I am a vegetarian," and you are sure there will be meatless dishes at dinner. However, when you sit at the table, you are faced with plates of sausage, jellied chicken, layered fish salad, and cabbage stuffed with rice and meat. As your host mother starts to serve you, you again say, "I'm a vegetarian." She looks at you blankly for a moment and continues to serve you large portions of meat and there are no vegetarian options available.

Question 3: Tell us how you might respond in situations where you have no control over the food you are offered to eat and people in your community serve you meat.

Appendix I

Romantic Involvement Worksheet

This worksheet is a tool for Peace Corps applicants who are currently involved in a significant romantic relationship to assess their readiness for Peace Corps service. The content and questions aim to educate and prepare applicants for the challenges related to the separation from a significant other that are unique to Peace Corps service. This is not meant as a selection tool for service. In order for this worksheet to be effective, it is important for you to have a frank discussion with your significant other about the impact of Peace Corps service on your relationship.

As a volunteer, you will face challenges related to leaving behind your partner beyond the mere twenty-seven-month separation. First, you must consider that at times during your Peace Corps service you will encounter a great deal of stress, transition, and isolation. The stress of an intensive training program and challenge of adapting to different cultural values may prove particularly difficult without the support of your partner. You may feel an overwhelming loss of friendship, love, and support at a time when you need it most.

Second, regular and reliable means of communications are not available to many Peace Corps volunteers. In many cases, mail takes two to four weeks for delivery and is not always reliable. This is often the only available means of communication with family and friends back home. All visits from friends and family must coincide with the volunteer's vacation. Volunteers can neither take vacation time during the first six months nor the last three months of service.

Finally, Peace Corps service tends to be a time of tremendous personal growth. Your perspective on many things will likely change as you experience life in another culture. Often returning home requires as much adjustment as adjusting to a new country and culture. This can also be a challenge for romantic relationships.

In order to best prepare you and your partner, please carefully consider, discuss, and answer the following questions. Please note, there are no right or wrong answers.

How significant do you consider your relationship?

Have you ever been separated during this relationship? If so, for how long?

How did you communicate during this time? How often did you visit each other?

Does your significant other support your decision to serve in the Peace Corps? If no, why not?

What are your future expectations for this relationship? What impact do you think Peace Corps service might have on your relationship?

What were the challenges identified by you as a couple? What strategies will you use to overcome the difficulties associated with separation from your significant other?

Appendix J

Joining Peace Corps as a Couple

The Application Process

- The application process for couples can be lengthy; expect it to take about ten to twelve months from the time that you submit your applications to the time that you depart for your country of service. Do not, however, apply more than twelve months in advance of the date you are available to leave.

- Because placements for married couples are limited, couples must be as flexible as possible. The more open you are to different regions of the world, as well as to different types of work assignments, the faster you will proceed through the application process.

- Narrow geographical preferences cannot be accommodated. Opportunities for volunteers are determined by the skills and educational backgrounds requested by host countries for specific assignment sites. Often one or both spouses will need to change their ideas about the type of work they'll do in order to fit into available assignment combinations. Again, the more flexible you are, the easier and quicker it will be to find a placement for you!

- Over half the couple assignments require either one year of college French or two years of college Spanish. We encourage you to enroll in either language, especially French, at a local community college in order to increase your competitiveness. If one person in the couple has some French or Spanish, we encourage the other person in the couple to enroll in that same language so both of you can reach a similar language level. Recruiters can often recommend you for a program contingent upon your completion of a language class.

Eligibility

- Each partner must qualify individually in order for a couple to be considered eligible to serve together.

- Couples must be married for at least six months prior to departure. A marriage certificate will be required.

- Families cannot be accommodated overseas. If a couple has dependents, they must provide proof that their children's needs will be met while they are away.

Appendix K

Volunteering at Age 50+

MEDICAL AND HEALTH INSURANCE

Will my medical expenses be covered while I am serving as a Volunteer?
The Peace Corps provides a comprehensive health program beginning at the start of Peace Corps service and continuing until you end service. This coverage includes health education and instruction, treatment for injuries/medical conditions, prescriptions, immunizations, and dental care. These services are delivered by the Peace Corps medical officer and/or other approved providers in-country.

What about after Peace Corps service is over?
After service, returned volunteers are eligible for eighteen months of coverage by a private health insurance called CorpsCare. Peace Corps pays the first month's premium and you have the option to purchase a comprehensive health insurance policy to cover you and qualified dependents. If you have service-related conditions that need an evaluation, your medical officer or the Office of Medical Services at headquarters will provide an authorization for this evaluation. If an illness or injury was related to your activities as a volunteer, you may be eligible for benefits under the Federal Employees' Compensation Act (FECA) through the Department of Labor.

Should I maintain my health insurance during Peace Corps service?
Some private sector retirees may experience difficulty in reapplying for health insurance upon completion of service. For this reason, private sector retirees may wish to consider maintaining their existing health insurance during service. Federal retirees may suspend federal employee health benefits during Peace Corps service. However, you will need to talk with your retirement officer to ensure that the suspension is done in a way that permits reenrollment.

The Peace Corps provides volunteers with full health care coverage during service, so check with your Medicare office to find out whether Medicare payments will continue to be deducted from your Social Security payment while you serve.

FINANCE

Will Peace Corps service affect my Social Security retirement benefits?
Only the Social Security Administration (SSA) can determine whether, or how, your benefits will be affected while you serve as a Peace Corps volunteer. The Peace Corps readjustment allowance (accrued at the rate of $225 per month and paid at the end of service for all months including training) and a small percentage of the monthly living allowance you are provided by the Peace Corps constitute

earnings for Social Security purposes. Social Security and Medicare tax payments are deducted from your monthly readjustment allowance.

How can I best maintain my home and financial affairs while overseas?

You may want to discuss with an attorney the possibility of giving a relative or friend power of attorney to handle your financial matters while you are serving in the Peace Corps. If you decide to rent your home while you are overseas, a property manager may be useful to arrange leases, handle rental income, pay taxes and insurance, and supervise needed repairs and maintenance on your home. You might also consider having an accountant or tax service prepare your income taxes while you are overseas.

WHILE SERVING ABROAD

Should I be anxious about learning a new language?

This is the number one concern of older applicants. Integration into your community is essential to being an effective Peace Corps volunteer, and communication is certainly a key element to that integration. To prepare you as a volunteer, Peace Corps' language-training teams provide approximately three months of training in-country by native speakers. This formal language training focuses on both grammar and overall communication skills. Trainees also typically live with a host family during their training, which provides an "immersion experience," enhancing language acquisition, cross-cultural adjustment, and assimilation into the community. Volunteers who need additional language instruction after pre-service training often arrange for a local tutor once they arrive at their work site. Additionally, many people find it helpful to begin a basic language course before they depart for service.

Are there any Peace Corps countries where volunteers are not sent due to age?

Placement is based on matching the skills of a volunteer with the needs of the host country as well as an assessment of a volunteer's medical needs and the appropriate services available in that country. A few countries have mandated retirement ages.

Index

About the Author

Dillon Banerjee served as an agroforestry volunteer in the Peace Corps from 1994 to 1996 in Belo, Cameroon. He received a B.A. from the College of William and Mary in Williamsburg, Virginia, where he studied political science and international economics. He earned an M.A. in International Development from the American University in Washington, D.C., and an Executive Masters in Sustainable Energy Systems from MIT's post-graduate program in Portugal. After returning from the Peace Corps, he worked at the U.S. Environmental Protection Agency in San Francisco, and the U.S. Agency for International Development in Washington, D.C., and Pretoria, South Africa. Dillon now serves as the director of the U.S. Embassy's International Trade program in Lisbon. He is married and has two children.